Creating a Successful Graphic Design Portfolio

Irina Lee

T0398392

BLOOMSBURY VISUAL ARTS
LONDON · NEW YORK · OXFORD · NEW DELHI · SYDNEY

BLOOMSBURY VISUAL ARTS
Bloomsbury Publishing Plc
50 Bedford Square, London, WC1B 3DP, UK
1385 Broadway, New York, NY 10018, USA

BLOOMSBURY, BLOOMSBURY VISUAL ARTS and the Diana
logo are trademarks of Bloomsbury Publishing Plc

First published in Great Britain 2021

For legal purposes the Acknowledgments on p. 193
constitute an extension of this copyright page.

Cover design: Louise Dugdale

A catalogue record for this book is available from the British Library.

Library of Congress Cataloging-in-Publication Data
Names: Lee, Irina, author.
Title: Creating a successful graphic design portfolio / Irina Lee.
Description: London ; New York : Bloomsbury Visual Arts, 2021. | Series:
Creative careers | Includes bibliographical references and index.
Identifiers: LCCN 2020011775 (print) | LCCN 2020011776 (ebook) | ISBN
9781474213875 (paperback) | ISBN 9781350031999 (epub) | ISBN
9781474213882 (pdf)
Subjects: LCSH: Art portfolios—Design. | Design services—Marketing.
Classification: LCC NC1001 .L44 2020 (print) | LCC NC1001 (ebook) | DDC
741.6023—dc23
LC record available at https://lccn.loc.gov/2020011775
LC ebook record available at https://lccn.loc.gov/2020011776

ISBN: PB: 978-1-4742-1387-5
ePDF: 978-1-4742-1388-2
eBook: 978-1-3500-3199-9

Series: Creative Careers

Typeset by Lachina Creative, Inc.
Printed and bound in India

To find out more about our authors and books visit
www.bloomsbury.com and sign up for our newsletters.

For Avery and Everett

Introduction

There is a gap between what the university teaches and what the design industry requires. The current industry discussion on what makes a perfect portfolio typically neglects career development advice. Many graduates come out of school and have a tough time understanding how to price themselves in the job market or how to network, as well as lacking the necessary skills to successfully transition to a design professional.

This book aims to strike a balance between offering practical advice on portfolio and career development. This advice is complemented by views and commentary from practicing design professionals. *Creating a Successful Graphic Design Portfolio* is a reference guide for graphic design students, graduates, and young professionals with three or less years of experience.

Creating a Successful Graphic Design Portfolio offers inspiration to young designers seeking advice, information, and encouragement. The book focuses on practical aspects of creating a great portfolio, getting feedback, what people look for in a portfolio, presenting yourself, dealing with criticism, interviewing for a design job, approaching the design exercise during an interview, tough interview questions, and starting a great career while balancing personal projects.

Design professionals will reflect on their design career and give advice throughout the book. Look for *Tip corners* throughout the book to read the professionals' advice, which will focus on a variety of different issues loosely grouped into topics like networking, work/life balance, money, mentorship, failing, freelancing and taxes, developing proposals, pricing, running a design studio, finding work, interviewing, maneuvering through office dynamics, and more.

Creating a Successful Graphic Design Portfolio

The book features a *Portfolio Clinic* (chapter 3). This section features samples from young designers' portfolios accompanied by design experts' evaluation, feedback, as well as advice to the reader on what works in this portfolio and areas of improvement. The range of featured portfolios (both print and digital) gives a full breadth of work and helpful evaluation and commentary by design professionals. Each portfolio review in this section is accompanied by tip boxes, colophons of fonts used, production details, vendors, special printing techniques used, software/tools used to build the digital prototypes, etc. This is designed to help the reader use the portfolios as models and reference points for their own pursuits.

Likewise, the book offers three additional clinic sections: *Resume*, *Cover letter*, and *Interview clinic*. These sections will include advice on writing an effective resume and cover letter geared towards the design industry, as well as sample prompts for answers to frequently asked questions during an interview.

Finally, the *Toolbox* section is a quick go-to reference guide that the reader can use throughout his or her career. This section will include templates for applying for a job, thank you and follow-ups, cover letters, and accepting or declining an offer as well as setting up informal interviews with prospective clients or employers to review your portfolio (not necessarily in response to a particular job post).

Suitable for any student starting out in design school, or young designer looking for perspective, *Creating a Successful Graphic Design Portfolio* provides a comprehensive survey of the graphic design market and career options. The content in this visual guide are supplemented with tips on portfolio presentation, training, design specialties, job search, tables outlining different industry opportunities, and salaries as well as business information, resources, professional associations, and sample templates. This book can sit on any designer's desk as easy reference, advice, and guidance. It's a reference you can use during your college years, and after.

This book talks about design and making it in the industry and focuses on integrity, presence, confidence, inspiration, and staying connected to the world.

1

I graduated. Now what?

You graduated and got your diploma. Now what? Is your portfolio good enough? How do you apply for a job? How do you know when and where to pick up freelance work? What IS freelance work? Keep reading if you want to be successful.

The transition from design student to design professional

Most design schools teach general practice, typography fundamentals, and fundamental design principles. Different media have different requirements. Editorial design is not the same as advertising: advertising is not the same as book design. Each has a unique focus and target. In most cases, the tools are similar but the methodologies and application are not.

Professional designers perform a broad range of tasks, switching media as clients and jobs demand. A designer cannot always afford to specialize because the volume of work in a specialty may not warrant it or competition may be too high.

Therefore, it's important, at the outset of a design career, to learn and gain internship experience (practice) in all the disciplines that interest you as well as those offering opportunities in future employment. Be fluent in as many forms as possible, rather than looking for a career niche—you can develop that later down the road.

Ask the professionals: How I got started

Carving my path

What was your first job in the design industry?

"I had a bunch of temp office jobs where I ended up designing all the presentations, flyers, and other miscellaneous things because people recognized I was good at it. I cobbled together a website portfolio of my work and landed at a small boutique agency as an Art Director, my first official design title! The focus was on digital, so I did a ton of website design." **Lara McCormick, Freelance Creative Director, San Francisco, California**

"Designer, WYD Design, 2 years, Westport, CT. My first job was at a small design studio called WYD design. They were doing award winning work and winning clients from some of the better known studios in the city. I worked there for a couple years doing print work, branding and annual reports. The art of annual reports was a great place to begin my career. The front part of the books were highly conceptual design which told the story of the company's year and future vision. The back part of the book was all about precision and good design systems with a nice dose of charts and infographics. They were the best of simple storytelling and design systems in service of a brand.

I find these broad skills translated easily for me as the landscape of design changed rapidly over the years. I learned to contribute through the full design process from concepts to mechanical setup, production and press proofing. This work taught me to juggle the different aspects of delivery of a complete book on time and without error. There was significant value placed on the details and perfection of craft. It set the standards and a way of working that I carry with me today." **Kris Kiger, Executive Vice President, Executive Creative Director, Design, R/GA, New York, New York**

"Something I've realized only after decades of working is that I was designing long before I had design in my title. In college, I worked for the school newspaper. While I thought of myself as a writer and editor, I actually designed those pages every week and learned a lot of my initial understanding of layout, print and information design from that.

But my first 'real' design job came much later as an interaction designer at Digitas NY, where I worked for

3.5 years. I mainly focused on wireframes, flows, and specs at first but by the end of my tenure, creatively led projects day to day." **Emily Wengert, Group Vice President, User Experience, Huge, Brooklyn, New York**

"Assistant Designer
Vintage Books (Random House)
NYC
1984–1985
I worked for the trade paperback imprint, Vintage Books, for a little over a year after graduating from SVA in 1984. I designed the backs of book covers, trafficked other designers covers, and got to design a few covers myself. I learned to do reasonably good mechanicals, to spec type, and I got to go on press to approve covers quite a few times." **Gail Anderson, Chair, BFA Design and BFA Advertising, Creative Director, Visual Arts Press, School of Visual Arts, New York, New York**

"Junior Graphic Designer
HZDG
5 years
I designed everything under the sun: advertisements, annuals, identities, and more." **Ida Woldemichael, Associate Creative Director, Wide Eye, Washington D.C.**

"Copywriter, Young & Rubicam (Y&R) Lisbon, 4 years, developing conceptual work for local and international (in 1991)." **Fred Saldanha, Global Chief Creative Officer, VMLY&R, New York, New York**

"Visual Designer, Quokka Sports 1998–2000, San Francisco
Visual designer for immersive sports media company focused on delivering realtime news, data, audio, video and telemetry. Was responsible for designing near-real-time interactive content for race viewers for motorsports, sailing races, and other dynamic content for events." **Ryan Scott Tandy, Product Design Manager, Instagram, San Francisco, California**

What was your favorite and least favorite part of your first job, and what was the most important thing you learned in that job?

"I loved the challenge of getting a creative brief with a design problem, going away for a day, and coming back with a design solution(s). I hated having to incorporate

13

14

client changes that I didn't believe in, but quickly learned to let things go and not to take anything personal." **Lara McCormick, Freelance Creative Director, San Francisco, California**

"My favorite part of that first job was learning to collaborate and deliver a body of work with a tight group of super talented people. I also really loved the process of creating. It was early days of adding computers into the flow and I adored the more analog hands on creation process.

I have very little complaints, but looking back, I hated how rudimentary the early digital tools were. It was a lot of unnecessary waiting and patience needed with them. I see what's possible now and I am astounded. The rate of change has been amazing and the reach that is possible to connect up, inspire, be inspired, share and collaborate is exponential.

I also learned how much better I became through my ability to work with others and collaborate. I think my first job taught me how to really work well and set my standards. It was that first experience that I recognized what kind of work I wanted to stand for and what kind of leader and director I wanted to be." **Kris Kiger, Executive Vice President, Executive Creative Director, Design, R/GA, New York, New York**

"I loved sitting next to the best designers and watching them work, trying to study all the quick keys and asking them why they were exploring certain paths. From that, I learned that I needed my on-screen design speed to match how fast I thought about the problem. I'd also create a million variations (or maybe just 20), and then only show my top 3. Learning how to cull down and what makes work strong or not is in many ways the true challenge of design.

The hardest part of my first job was the career reset and being at the bottom of the food chain again. I'd worked as a journalist and in book publishing for 5 years. When I switched, I was back to the beginning. That meant getting all the worst assignments: like 120-page design specs naming every cut graphic and every line of copy. I still shudder!" **Emily Wengert, Group Vice President, User Experience, Huge, Brooklyn, New York**

"The art director I worked for never had a design assistant before and she didn't give me much direction. But I shared my office with her office manager and we had a lot of fun, and listened to a lot of cassettes

(that's how long ago it was). The best part of the job was swapping stories with the other design assistants from Knopf and Pantheon, and to get to know the fabulous Louise Fili, who was the art director at Pantheon at the time." **Gail Anderson, Chair, BFA Design and BFA Advertising, Creative Director, Visual Arts Press, School of Visual Arts, New York, New York**

"Favorite: The variety of work, from the client type to deliverable type.

Least favorite: Getting files production ready. Most important thing I learned: talk to your peers about your work and be open to feedback" **Ida Woldemichael, Associate Creative Director, Wide Eye, Washington D.C.**

"I loved the amount of new problems I had to solve every day. But I suffered from the fear of failure. What you learn is that failure is part of the process, and makes us better professionals." **Fred Saldanha, Global Chief Creative Officer, VMLY&R, New York, New York**

"I was surrounded by designers infinitely more talented and experienced than I was. I learned so much every day. The hardest part was the fact that the websites we created operated in near-real time 24-hours a day documenting these epic sport experiences. This mean working insane hours producing interactive content, sleeping under our desks during production, and working with some pretty demanding sponsors who always wanted more prominent branding." **Ryan Scott Tandy, Product Design Manager, Instagram, San Francisco, California**

What advice would you give on transitioning from a design student to an entry-level professional?

"When you're fresh out of school it can be daunting and feel very competitive. It's easy to compare yourself to other designers when you first start out (compare and despair!). Instead, be yourself, stay positive, and know that you'll land exactly where you are supposed to. And if that first job doesn't match the ideal you have in your head, know that it's not permanent and just a stepping stone to your next role. Learn as much as you can before you move on." **Lara McCormick, Freelance Creative Director, San Francisco, California**

"Keep your eyes wide open.

Learn everything you can about the work and culture you're in. You will become part of it and help shape it by being present.

Learn from the best and the worst of your experiences.

Your career will be long. It's a pursuit and a life-long love affair.

Know what you don't know and be excited to find out. Be truly curious and unafraid to ask questions. Become good at listening to the answers

Great basic design principles apply.

Build on them. Everything you gain in design will carry forward and translate to the new. You are cumulative.

Seek out the context of things and develop a love of empathy.

These two things will be the most important tools to help you solve any design problem. Plus, the world just needs way more empathy, and context is essential in finding it." **Kris Kiger, Executive Vice President, Executive Creative Director, Design, R/GA, New York, New York**

"Try out ideas you hate. Just try them. You might be surprised.

Always bring an option you weren't asked to make.

Listen but always talk." **Emily Wengert, Group Vice President, User Experience, Huge, Brooklyn, New York**

"This sounds like a cliché, and perhaps it is, but it's increasingly foreign to students: Be the first one in the office and the last one to leave. Okay, not every single day, but *almost* every day. Your enthusiasm and desire to learn and be of assistance will not go unnoticed. And while you're at it, limit your texting and get back to work. And get off my lawn.

You have so much to learn, and if you're earnest and hard-working, you'll find some kind soul to mentor you, or to at least give you a proper heads up about office culture. They'll show you cool books and interesting typefaces, and will help keep you out of trouble.

When all else fails, bring in snacks." **Gail Anderson, Chair, BFA Design and BFA Advertising, Creative Director, Visual Arts Press, School of Visual Arts, New York, New York**

"Work for people and organizations you admire.

Consider their values and how they align with yours.

Have fun!

Remember that you bring your own special value, simply for being you." **Ida Woldemichael, Associate Creative Director, Wide Eye, Washington D.C.**

"Be curious. Be interesting. Do things you do not know how to do. Do not be afraid to fail. Be critical of yourself. Learn all about design. Be the greatest nerd in the design. Never choose the easy way out. Never switch jobs because of money. Do not give up when you receive bad feedback. Do not think good feedback solves everything. Always look for more. And most important of all: work with people you admire and with brands you love. Believe me, it's that simple." **Fred Saldanha, Global Chief Creative Officer, VMLY&R, New York, New York**

"Draw—Don't get stuck on the screen for everything you do. Make sketching a core part of your process, both while designing and in even in meetings.

Breathe—Remember that some projects succeed and others fail. It's ok to park certain ideas, learn from them, and move on.

Presentations—If you're not a strong public speaker get training so you can become one. Communicating your ideas is equally as important as creating them.

Inspiration—Always do your homework and look for inspiration from a broad range of sources as you start any project. Go deep on your subject area, and become an expert in knowing who you're designing for.

Joy—Remember that design always has the opportunity to create an emotional reaction; even if you're designing a postage stamp. It's the best part of this profession" **Ryan Scott Tandy, Product Design Manager, Instagram, San Francisco, California**

2

Your design career

Before you start your career, it's helpful to learn the lay of the land. What type of opportunities are out there? Of course, there are a bunch of different options, but here is a broad guide to the type of work a designer might expect to find in today's industry.

These options are mainly about full-time opportunities. There are also tons of full-time and part-time freelance and internship opportunities that we will cover later in the book.

An introduction to design opportunities

Questions to ask yourself

Focus

» Is your goal to work mainly in Graphic Design (Visual Design) or Interaction Design?

Industry

» Do you want to develop a domain expertise? (e.g., fashion, technology, media, healthcare, non-profit)?
» Do you want to work on a range of problems?

Medium

» Are you passionate about a particular medium (e.g., print, digital, motion, environments, integrated)?
» Do you want to specialize, or do you want to design for a variety of touchpoints?

Environment

» What kind of environment would best suit you (e.g., agency, design studio, in-house, startup, freelance)?
» What do you want to work on (e.g., product, service, marketing, research/strategy)?
» What is the ideal company size and stage for you?
» What is the design POV of the organization (e.g., house style, variety, user-centered)?
» Are you looking for autonomy, mentorship, or collaboration?
» Who do you want to work with on a daily basis (e.g., designers, other disciplines)?
» Do you want to work in a structured team or do you want a variety of collaborators?
» Do you want a variety of projects or to stay focused on a single client or problem?

Where to work and what to expect

Industry	Agency	Publishing	In-house marketing	In-house product
Overview	Agencies service different clients, where you might be part of a large team working on projects such as outdoor ads, television commercials, or digital products and websites.	You might be designing print editorial layouts for magazines, newspapers or other publications, or working on book jackets.	In-house marketing design focuses on creating design and collateral to promote a single brand or company.	In-house product designers focus solely on a single company's digital product. You might be designing, developing, or mocking up internal deliverables.
Example Jobs	Associate Designer at HUGE UX Designer at Wunderman Junior Experience Designer at R/GA Junior Designer at Hyperakt	Junior Designer at *New York Times* Designer at *Vogue Magazine* Book Designer at Penguin Books	Visual Designer at MercyCorp Associate Graphic Designer at Kate Spade Production Designer at HBO Junior Designer at United Nations	Junior Communications Designer at Facebook Junior Product Designer at iHeartRadio Visual Designer at Google
Pros and Cons	Pros: Exposure to many different industries and clients Opportunities to rotate to different accounts and possibly even different locations (if you work for a large agency) Cons: Long hours High pressure	Pros: See your work published and "out in the real world" Opportunities to collaborate with different illustrators, photographers, and lettering artists on various assignments Cons: Possibly less creative control on certain projects where the author or publisher may have the final say in the design Publishing companies come and go due to the shifting industry of publishing	Pros: Ability to understand a company's brand and work across its campaigns and digital products Opportunities to collaborate with vendors and advertising agencies Cons: Potentially less variety from working on the same brand Possibly less opportunities for campaigns, as many in-house marketing projects are bid out to agency partners	Pros: Learn how to test different layouts for content to see what will be the most effective solution Understanding of analytics and other measuring metrics on every interaction Cons: More constraint in design because you might have to stick with a predefined library of elements within your company's brand

Charting a design career

Career growth can take place in many different ways. At times, you may find your career taking a linear progression, and at other times, it may seem like a winding road. The important thing to remember is that there's no wrong or right way to grow in the design industry, as long as you feel professionally challenged and personally fulfilled.

This is a very general guide on what to expect in career growth (a.k.a. promotions) at different industries.*

*Generally speaking.

Agency (Visual Design focus)	Agency (User Experience focus)	Small Design Studio	In-House	Startup
Intern	Intern	Intern	Intern	Paths vary—largely tenure-based
↓	↓	↓	↓	
Junior Designer	Junior UX Designer	Designer	Designer	Roles aren't as defined; designers tend to wear many hats
↓	↓	↓	↓	
Designer	UX Designer	Art Director	Senior Designer	
↓	↓	↓	↓	
Senior Designer	Senior UX Designer	Creative Director	Art Director	
↓	↓	↓	↓	
Art Director	UX Lead	Partner	Creative Director	
↓	↓		↓	
Senior Art Director	UX Design Director		Executive Director	
↓	↓			
Associate Creative Director	Group UX Design Director			
↓	↓			
Creative Director	Executive UX Design Director			
↓				
Group Creative Director				
↓				
Executive Creative Director				

A few ideas on where to work

Traditional Agencies

Arnold Worldwide
BBDO
BBH
DDB
Deutsch
Droga 5
Goodby, Silverstein & Partners
JWT
MCCann
Ogilvy & Mather
Publicis
Saatchi & Saatchi
TBWA
Wieden + Kennedy

Digital Agencies

72 and Sunny
360i
AKQA
Anomaly
Barbarian
Big Spaceship
Firstborn
Huge
Instrument
Organic
R/GA
Rokkan
Sapient Razorfish
VML

Branding Agencies

Collins
FutureBrand
Interbrand
Landor
Lippincott
Method
Pentagram
Red Antler
Siegel + Gale
Sterling Brands
Wolff Olins

Consultancies

Deloitte
Frog Design
IDEO
Red Scout
Smart Design
SY Partners
?What If!

Publishing

Chronicle Books
Conde Nast
Hearst
New York Magazine
Penguin Books
The New York Times

Design Studios

2x4
Base
Hunter Gatherer
Hyperakt
Local Projects
MTWTF
Project Projects

In-House

Beauty
    Estee Lauder
    SKII
Culture
    MoMA
    Whitney Museum
E-Comm
    Amazon
    Etsy
    Jet.com
Education
    Lynda.com
    Skillshare
Entertainment
    Disney
    MTV
    Viacomm
Fashion
    COACH
    JCrew
    Kate Spade
Finance
    American Express
    Betterment
    Bloomberg
    JPMorgan Chase
Social Good
    American Red Cross
    Government Agencies
    UNICEF
Sports
    ESPN
    MLB
    MSL
    NBA
    NFL

Product and Technology

Apple
Facebook
Foursquare
Google
Intel
Kickstarter
Microsoft
Square
Twitter

Tip corner: Advice from recent graduates

My experience on making the jump

What school did you attend, and how did it prepare you for "the real world"?

"I attended the University of the Arts in Philadelphia, PA and graduated in 2015 with a BFA in graphic design. My school really focused on the foundations (and was heavily rooted in Swiss design), which became really useful when I started doing projects that were closer to things I'd encounter in the 'real world' like branding. The more I became comfortable with the foundation, the more I felt comfortable twisting and breaking the rules to create more interesting work. School is the absolute best time to experiment and make cool things! I also found that when I started to treat my school projects like they were for real clients, I was more invested in the outcomes which elevated the final outcome. I still use some of my school projects in my portfolio to this day, so it's important to be proud of the work that you're doing in school." **Anna Rising, Designer & Illustrator, Oslo, Norway (Class of 2015, BFA Graphic Design, University of the Arts in Philadelphia, Pennsylvania)**

"Right after graduating from high school, I came straight to New York City. I studied at the School of Visual Arts as an Advertising & Design major and graduated in May 2018. Throughout the my four years at SVA, I was presented with a lot of opportunities. I had the chance to learn under the instruction and brilliance of many creatives, who were all currently working and deeply immersed within the industry. This definitely gave me an upper hand in becoming more professional and well-versed with the workings within a studio/agency. They expected a lot out of me and I tried my very best to do so. I owe the successful kick-start of my career it to my professors, big time." **Ein Jung, Product Designer, Bunch, New York, New York (Class of 2018, BFA Advertising and Design, School of Visual Arts, New York, New York)**

"I attended the Maryland Institute College of Art (MICA) and graduated with an MFA in Graphic Design in 2016. I think my graduate education gave me a strong design foundation and that it allowed me to try out different aspects of design that I thought was interesting to me. Leaving school, I felt prepared to take on bigger projects while working with a multidisciplinary team. But let's be real here, as a designer, you are never done learning." **Hieu Tran, Product Designer, OpenSpace, San Francisco, California (Class of 2016, MFA Graphic Design, Maryland Institute College of Art, Baltimore, Maryland)**

"I graduated from the Rhode Island School of Design (RISD) in June 2017, with a BFA in graphic design. RISD did a good job in challenging me to think conceptually and to be scrappy—to adapt to dynamic situations, roll with the punches of criticism and feedback on my work, and to constantly make and iterate on tight deadlines. I don't come from a design background, and my education in school was my first exposure to the field of graphic design. It was at RISD I both learned the fundamentals and developed a passion for design." **Jason Fujikuni, Art Director, Brand Identity *The New York Times*, New York, New York (Class of 2017, BFA Graphic Design, Rhode Island School of Design, Providence, Rhode Island)**

"I attended Oklahoma State University. I graduated May 2017 and majored in Graphic Design with a minor in Marketing. Going into college, I had no idea what I wanted to do. I started out in Business, moved to Interior Design, and then last minute switched to graphic design after taking one drawing class. In my first design class, I realized that this was something I was going to love. Deadlines, late nights, critiques, these are all things I experienced in college, but still continue to experience out of it. Fortunately, I get paid for it now. But without those years of experience in college, I don't think I would have been prepared for the kind of work I do now. Also, learning to respect your professor and their advice both about your work and your future was huge in getting me where I am today.

If you can't respect your professors and trust that they have more knowledge than you, then you will never be able to respect and trust your Creative Director." **Julia Whitley, Graphic Designer, Barkley, Kansas City, Missouri (Class of 2017, BFA Graphic Design, Oklahoma State University, Stillwater, Oklahoma)**

"I attended the Rhode Island School of Design (RISD) for its graduate program in Graphic Design. This is a tricky question because I chose RISD precisely because it seemed to be more removed from the so-called 'real world' than some of the other schools I had considered. I thought that RISD's MFA program was less commercially minded, which I liked. One of the most helpful skills I honed at RISD is the ability to present ideas in effective and engaging ways." **June Shin, Type Designer, Occupant Fonts/Morisawa USA, Providence, Rhode Island (Class of 2017, MFA Graphic Design, Rhode Island School of Design, Providence, Rhode Island)**

"I graduated from the BFA Design program at the School of Visual Arts in 2016. Throughout my program, students were able to explore a wide variety of disciplines—including motion graphics, interaction design, classic print formats, 3-D design, and many more. This allowed me to dabble in different mediums that not only helped me figure out what I was truly interested in, but also shaped me into a multidisciplinary designer. Bringing a wide variety of skills to a job is something I have found my directors appreciate and have me continue to explore—which in turn keeps me learning and growing." **Linnea Taylor, Multimedia Designer, School of Visual Arts, New York, New York (Class of 2016, BFA Design, School of Visual Arts, New York, New York)**

"I was a design student at the School of Visual Arts, graduating class of 2016. While pursuing my undergraduate degree, I was commuting to school and took advantage of as many on-campus activities that I could participate in. My teachers and roles and responsibilities outside of the classroom shaped my work ethic that carried over into my professional career. Juggling full time classwork, part time internships, RA (resident assistant) responsibilities and designing the student run publication taught me time management and prioritization. Having smart teachers who challenged

my ability to problem solve also greatly impacted how I approach conceptualization." **Masha Vainblat, Senior Digital Designer at Steven Madden, LTD, Long Island City, New York (Class of 2016, BFA Design, School of Visual Arts, New York, New York)**

"I attended the School of Visual Arts (SVA) and graduated with my BFA in Graphic Design. The faculty there were incredibly supportive and resourceful in helping their students such as myself find different job opportunities and summer internships over the 4 years I studied at SVA. All the instructors I had in school are currently working in the industry so they are incredibly informative on how to navigate the real world of agencies, studios and client relationships. A vast majority of them have a network locally and internationally that connect their students and help lead them to jobs straight out of college." **Yejee Pae, Junior Designer, Communal Creative, New York, New York (Class of 2018, BFA Design, School of Visual Arts, New York, New York)**

What is your current profession and where do you work?

"I am currently working as a brand designer at Red Antler in Brooklyn, New York. I recently made the transition from working in the digital realm to the branding side of things, and also do a bit of illustration. When time permits, I like to take on some freelance work for some friends, and also like to work on my own side-projects. Lately, my side-projects have been focused in illustration." **Anna Rising, Designer & Illustrator, Oslo, Norway (Class of 2015, BFA Graphic Design, University of the Arts in Philadelphia, Pennsylvania)**

"I'm currently working at R/GA as an associate designer in New York City. I mainly help different teams with pitching ideas to clients, creating compelling stories and visuals to win their hearts over. In my spare time, I often work with my friends (photographers, cinematographers, painters, etc.) with branding themselves and presenting their portfolios." **Ein Jung, Product Designer, Bunch, New York, New York (Class of 2018, BFA Advertising and Design, School of Visual Arts)**

23

Tip corner: Advice from recent graduates

"Currently, I am a Designer at an early-stage startup called OpenSpace in San Francisco. I joined the startup as their first in-house designer where I spend about 25% of my time on brand design and the other 75% on product design. On the side, I try pick up smaller freelance gigs here and there—currently I am working on designing a mobile app for a start-up in New York City as well as working with the MIT School of Architecture and Planning on some recruitment collaterals." **Hieu Tran, Designer, OpenSpace, San Francisco, California (Class of 2016, MFA Graphic Design, Maryland Institute College of Art, Baltimore, Maryland)**

"I am a brand identity designer and digital art director at *The New York Times*. I design logos, style guides and identity systems for cross platform use across the *New York Times* newsroom and company, and commission illustration and help produce special, editorial projects." **Jason Fujikuni, Art Director, Brand Identity *The New York Times*, New York, New York (Class of 2017, BFA Graphic Design, Rhode Island School of Design, Providence, Rhode Island)**

"I am currently a graphic designer at Barkley, Kansas City, Missouri. I work within the Design and Experience department and primarily on clients such as Applebee's and IHOP. We do all of their in-store promotional materials as well as help on campaigns, internal events, and new ventures." **Julia Whitley, Graphic Designer, Barkley, Kansas City, Missouri (Class of 2017, BFA Graphic Design, Oklahoma State University, Stillwater, Oklahoma)**

"I currently work as a type designer for Occupant Fonts, a brand of Morisawa USA. I work out of a coworking design studio space in Providence called the Design Office. I use my evening hours and weekends to take on short-term graphic design and lettering projects. I am keen on maintaining my design practice on top of my full-time type design job." **June Shin, Type Designer, Occupant Fonts/Morisawa USA, Providence, Rhode Island (Class of 2017, MFA Graphic Design, Rhode Island School of Design, Providence, Rhode Island)**

"Currently, I am a Multimedia Designer in New York City at the School of Visual Art's in-house design studio, the Visual Arts Press. I started as an intern for the Web Design team, then graduated to a Front End Web Designer, until my current position. I split my time now between working on projects for both the print and web teams. For print jobs, I mostly work on collateral (such as invitations, posters, promotional brochures, etc.) for gallery shows, events, and various departments throughout the school. On the web side, we are in the middle of a massive redesign that I've been able to be a big part of by creating 100+ wireframes, coding interactive prototypes, and strategizing site-wide content reduction. Additionally, I create and code e-blast campaigns for various departments and institutional-wide events." **Linnea Taylor, Multimedia Designer, School of Visual Arts, New York, New York (Class of 2016, BFA Design, School of Visual Arts, New York, New York)**

"Currently I am a designer and producer at Steve Madden. Our headquarters are located in Long Island City, NY. I got my foot in the door by taking an opportunity starting as the marketing assistant. My hard work and willingness to express my strengths enabled me to grow into and create my current title. What I learned from the marketing role now carries over and strengthens my ability to bridge the creative and marketing needs at Steve Madden. I used to freelance as a web designer but put that on hold to create a work/life balance and focus on my personal passion projects like my crochet-wear business." **Masha Vainblat, Senior Digital Designer at Steven Madden, LTD, Long Island City, New York (Class of 2016, BFA Design, School of Visual Arts, New York, New York)**

"As a newly graduated student, my OPT visa has been processed and I recently started as a Junior Designer at a small design studio called Communal Creative. I work on projects that range from package design, site design, and printed matter; and I also work alongside my art director in flushing out full identity systems for new clients that come underway." **Yejee Pae, Junior Designer, Communal Creative, New York, New York (Class of 2018, BFA Design, School of Visual Arts, New York, New York)**

What are some of the exciting aspects of your occupation and career?

"Variety! I love being a designer because my skills can translate over a multitude of different mediums. I'm constantly working on new brands and projects, and have yet to find myself bored. I've also come across some projects where I'm doing stuff I never thought I'd be paid to do—like creating ridiculous memes or Photoshopping monkeys in subway cars. As cheesy as it sounds, design is constantly changing and there really are endless opportunities to try new things." **Anna Rising, Designer & Illustrator, Oslo, Norway (Class of 2015, BFA Graphic Design, University of the Arts in Philadelphia, Pennsylvania)**

"The People! The Work! It's always exciting to be surrounded by others who are creatively charged and looking for ways to release their energy." **Ein Jung, Product Designer, Bunch, New York, New York (Class of 2018, BFA Advertising and Design, School of Visual Arts, New York, New York)**

"I think the most exciting aspect of my career is the challenge of working with a group of people toward a common goal. Other cool things include: learning about the topic/industry based on the projects, trying out new design tools, and reading designers' reactions on brand re-brands :D." **Hieu Tran, Product Designer, OpenSpace, San Francisco, California (Class of 2016, MFA Graphic Design, Maryland Institute College of Art, Baltimore, Maryland)**

"One of my favorite aspects about design is that it is collaborative. Working at The Times is an incredibly humbling and exciting experience because I am constantly meeting and collaborating with intelligent, kind, passionate and diverse people both within and outside of the company. I feel privileged and grateful to say that I am constantly learning on the job, and that is part of what makes it most dynamic and engaging for me." **Jason Fujikuni, Art Director, Brand Identity** *The New York Times*, **New York, New York (Class of 2017, BFA Graphic Design, Rhode Island School of Design, Providence, Rhode Island)**

"Barkley is a super innovative company. In fact, our goal is to become the number one creative idea company, so our leadership is very open to new ideas and actually promotes us trying to push our clients to new levels. We also have a lot of cool perks such as a wine tap, beer fridge, zen rooms, and the opportunity to take 3 work days and learn a new skill on the company's dime. My team also does a lot of the photography for our clients so there is hope that one day I will be able to go on some photo shoots in California." **Julia Whitley, Graphic Designer, Barkley, Kansas City, Missouri (Class of 2017, BFA Graphic Design, Oklahoma State University, Stillwater, Oklahoma)**

"Type is everywhere. Whether we realize it or not, it affects how we experience the world. It is exciting to know that as a type and graphic designer I am contributing to how our culture looks and feels in some ways, however small they may be. The bonus perk is that I get to travel fairly often to attend conferences, which are a lot of fun." **June Shin, Type Designer, Occupant Fonts/Morisawa USA, Providence, Rhode Island (Class of 2017, MFA Graphic Design, Rhode Island School of Design, Providence, Rhode Island)**

"The most exciting aspects of my career are the variety of the projects I work on, along with the freedom I am given to create them. Although my focus is mostly web and print, my directors have trusted me with an assortment of assignments that let me explore mediums I'm not as familiar with. For example, I didn't pursue video filming or editing much, but I've had the chance to create video and motion content for our social media accounts, full video series for YouTube and Vimeo, and theatre displays and projections for large events. I am a person who likes to be challenged and to learn new things, so whatever they throw at me I am excited to be able to explore and create something I never imagined I could." **Linnea Taylor, Multimedia Designer, School of Visual Arts, New York, New York (Class of 2016, BFA Design, School of Visual Arts, New York, New York)**

Tip corner: Advice from recent graduates

"Working so closely with the marketing and creative teams opens the door to attend photo shoots and promotional events. We have photo shoots almost every week and I even got to meet Cardi B during our collaboration. I've had the opportunity to be a leg model in some of our social and global campaigns. Also, free shoes! It's almost every girl's dream. But one of the best things about working at Steve Madden is my team. It's really like family." **Masha Vainblat, Senior Digital Designer at Steven Madden, LTD, Long Island City, New York (Class of 2016, BFA Design, School of Visual Arts, New York, New York)**

"The most exciting part about being in a studio environment is that it is such a collaborative and encouraging atmosphere. I personally hated working in isolation throughout my sophomore to senior year at SVA (School of Visual Arts), and I wished that college provided more opportunities to collaborate with students. What I love about working at Communal Creative is that the studio was founded by a woman and it is still uncommon in the design industry to find studios that are not male dominated. It is refreshing and empowering to be working in an environment like this, and generally speaking, I love working for real clients because the reward is so much higher than just having a completed project in a book, and it feels great as a newly graduated student to finally get paid to do something that I enjoy doing." **Yejee Pae, Junior Designer, Communal Creative, New York, New York (Class of 2018, BFA Design, School of Visual Arts, New York, New York)**

What career advice would you share with aspiring designers or current design students?

"Never stop creating your own work and never stop doing what you love outside of design. I can confidently say that my side projects are the reason I'm at the place in my career that I'm at. In all of my phone calls and interviews with prospective jobs, my work that came out of a place of passion was always the work that was seen the most successful. And for your own sanity and mental health, keep up with your hobbies and passions outside of design! Being able to step out of your design headspace into something else that you love is the best way to restart your brain and get fresh perspectives." **Anna Rising, Designer & Illustrator, Oslo, Norway (Class of 2015, BFA Graphic Design, University of the Arts in Philadelphia, Pennsylvania)**

"The best kind of opportunities present themselves to those who are confident and are prepared. Be comfortable with discussing your projects and ideas. Always be eager to learn and experience more. And stop comparing yourself to others!" **Ein Jung, Product Designer, Bunch, New York, New York (Class of 2018, BFA Advertising and Design, School of Visual Arts, New York, New York)**

"Don't be too picky in the beginning and be grateful for any kind of opportunities. Also—be bold, take risks, don't be afraid of failures, embrace the unknown. And it's okay to cry sometimes :)" **Hieu Tran, Product Designer, OpenSpace, San Francisco, California (Class of 2016, MFA Graphic Design, Maryland Institute College of Art, Baltimore, Maryland)**

"*'Zoom in,'* meaning, pay attention to the details and hone in on what you are passionate about." **Jason Fujikuni, Art Director, Brand Identity** *The New York Times***, New York, New York (Class of 2017, BFA Graphic Design, Rhode Island School of Design, Providence, Rhode Island)**

"My career advice would be to start your online presence early in college. My bosses all look for people's behance or their website before even giving an initial interview, so if your work isn't out there for people to see, they may miss you. A lot of my classmates weren't prepared to apply for jobs until months after we graduated and that can hurt more than help. I would also tell aspiring designers to not be afraid to take work out of their portfolio. Not everything you make is going to be up to the standards of your best work, so it is better to have less great pieces rather than a lot of okay work. Being able to curate your own work shows potential employers that you have a good eye for what good design is." **Julia Whitley, Graphic Designer, Barkley, Kansas City, Missouri (Class of 2017, BFA Graphic Design, Oklahoma State University, Stillwater, Oklahoma)**

"Don't be afraid to ask for what you want. You'd be surprised how often people say yes. Even if it's a no, what have you got to lose?" **June Shin, Type Designer, Occupant Fonts/Morisawa USA, Providence, Rhode Island (Class of 2017, MFA Graphic Design, Rhode Island School of Design, Providence, Rhode Island)**

"Honestly, I've always been a person of simple means so my goals have never been driven by fame, money, or anything of that nature. I love what I do, so my goals are to keep creating with a team that I care about, and in turn appreciates me, for an institution or company that I believe is doing good work for the right causes. Of course being able to pay the bills and more is a nice feeling, but understand your limitations. The worst thing you can do is be a young artist that burns yourself out so fast that you don't enjoy creating anymore. Right now, I am super happy where I am and find fulfillment from the work I am making, so I'm focusing on that and seeing where it takes me. (However, I will say that I'm a fangirl of the fourth estate so one day being able to work with or for NPR would be super sick—support your local public radio station!)" **Linnea Taylor, Multimedia Designer, School of Visual Arts, New York, New York (Class of 2016, BFA Design, School of Visual Arts, New York, New York)**

"Know your worth, be fearless enough to seek opportunities and always always always stay humble." **Masha Vainblat, Senior Digital Designer at Steven Madden, LTD, Long Island City, New York (Class of 2016, BFA Design, School of Visual Arts, New York, New York)**

"Something I discovered and was refreshingly reminded of during college is that I am a human being who also happens to be a designer. I need other things I do in my life other than design in order to feel sane and happy. Find out for yourself what it is you love doing. If it is design, then that's great but you must find a balance between your career and every other aspect of your life, because at the end of the day, our career is not (or should not) consume our entire lives. . . that's just me though." **Yejee Pae, Junior Designer, Communal Creative, New York, New York (Class of 2018, BFA Design, School of Visual Arts, New York, New York)**

Mapping out your career path

Do you know what you want in your career? Where do you want to be? What do you want to do? What is your dream job? The only want to find out is to set a vision and prepare yourself by researching what's out there so you can make the informed decisions when it comes to your career.

Be clear on what you want to do, and where you want to go. Roman philosopher Seneca reminds us, "Luck is what happens when preparation meets opportunity." The difference between being lucky and unlucky is your perspective. Luck isn't only about being at the right place at the right time, it's about being prepared, open and ready for opportunities. Being prepared will give you the advantage to make thoughtful decisions, so instead of jumping from job to job, you can make strategic decisions to help you navigate to your goal.

Use the worksheet below to write down your goals.

MY CAREER PATH WORKSHEET

Section 1: My career objectives and goals
First, write down your career objectives. Be deliberate. You may want to begin by writing down many different options and then edit and revise. This step is extremely important.

_____
_____
_____
_____
_____

Great! Now, for the second step, write down your top 4 dream companies. For each company, write down the name, location, and what they do.

_____
_____
_____
_____
_____

Section 2: Research
Next, research the design industry. Start by reading the section, *An introduction to design opportunities*, filled with resources to help you get oriented with the design industry and career possibilities.

After you read the *An introduction to design opportunities* section, continue to research other companies that sparked your interest. Look for different industries that interest you (e.g., interaction design, architecture firms, fashion industry, editorial design, small agencies, big agencies, startups, book publishers, museums, non-profits, etc.). Look at different locations (e.g., New York City, California, Portland, Midwest, Europe, London, Amsterdam, etc.). Organize your research and group them by industry and/or location. Research a minimum of 100 places, but you should have many more options. 100 is just a start!

_____
_____
_____
_____
_____

Section 3: My professional network

Next, create a LinkedIn account. Populate your professional profile: upload a professional picture, write an objective, employment history, education, honors, etc. Use LinkedIn to research your top picks from your list of 100+. Research a minimum of 15 designers who currently work at those companies. Again, 15 is just a start. Review their online portfolios. Save/download their work that you think best represents the kind of work you'll need to have in your portfolio to get hired. Be sure to organize your files and save the sources/credits. Now you know what type of work you need to get to your dream job. If you're feeling brave, connect to those designers and ask to set up an informal portfolio review to get feedback on your work.

_____
_____
_____
_____
_____
_____

Section 4: My portfolio assessment

Now that you've researched your dream companies and seen the type of work that it takes to get there, assess your current portfolio. Hopefully, you also met with design professionals to get feedback on your current portfolio. Which pieces are most appropriate for the type of job you want? Identify the gaps you'll need to fill. Act on the gaps. Create ideas, comps, and sketches.

Note: You will have a chance to develop these sketches and get these pieces interview-ready. For the purpose of this worksheet, it's important to see that you identify gaps in your current portfolio and take initial steps in creating the missing work that you think you'll need to get the job you want.

Write down a list of work you'll need to have in your portfolio in order to get hired at your dream jobs. This can be informed by the work you collected from your research.

_____
_____
_____
_____
_____

Review your current portfolio. Identify 4–5 pieces that you think are appropriate to include in order to get your dream job. Write down which portfolio pieces you'll keep.

_____
_____
_____
_____
_____

Identify the gaps and weaknesses you have to fill in your current portfolio. Sketch what portfolio pieces you'd like to develop further to get your dream job.

29

Tip corner: Advice from recent graduates

My career goals

What are your ultimate long-term career goals?

"I would really love to start my own studio or practice one day. I think it's really empowering when I get to lead projects and work directly with clients, and aspire to get to a place where I can be choosy about the projects that I take on." **Anna Rising, Designer & Illustrator, Oslo, Norway (Class of 2015, BFA Graphic Design, University of the Arts in Philadelphia, Pennsylvania)**

"One day I hope to open my own studio. Or maybe become a theatrical set designer. Wherever life decides to takes me!" **Ein Jung, Product Designer, Bunch, New York, New York (Class of 2018, BFA Advertising and Design, School of Visual Arts, New York, New York)**

"I am at interesting point of my career right now where I am slowing transitioning from a Visual Designer to a Product Designer. I am hoping to join a startup within the next year, and eventually work my way up to become a design director. Along the way, I would love to go back into teaching because I think it is important to give back to the design community by passing on what I know to the younger designers." **Hieu Tran, Product Designer, OpenSpace, San Francisco, California (Class of 2016, MFA Graphic Design, Maryland Institute College of Art, Baltimore, Maryland)**

"I have always had a passion for, the so-called, design for social good—for me, that would mean the opportunity to do design work that is not just aesthetic, but involves strategy and problem solving to bring people together and to support a cause. Many of my mentors are both design professionals and educators, and I would love to have the opportunity to teach and mentor young designers." **Jason Fujikuni, Art Director, Brand Identity** *The New York Times*, **New York, New York (Class of 2017, BFA Graphic Design, Rhode Island School of Design, Providence, Rhode Island)**

"One of my ultimate long-term career goals is to own my own design studio. I studied entrepreneurship initially in college, so owning my own business is still something that resonates with me." **Julia Whitley, Graphic Designer, Barkley, Kansas City, Missouri (Class of 2017, BFA Graphic Design, Oklahoma State University, Stillwater, Oklahoma)**

"I choose not to make long-term goals. I focus on doing what I actually enjoy in the present. That has served me well." **June Shin, Type Designer, Occupant Fonts/Morisawa USA, Providence, Rhode Island (Class of 2017, MFA Graphic Design, Rhode Island School of Design, Providence, Rhode Island)**

"Honestly, I've always been a person of simple means so my goals have never been driven by fame, money, or anything of that nature. I love what I do, so my goals are to keep creating with a team that I care about, and in turn appreciates me, for an institution or company that I believe is doing good work for the right causes. Of course being able to pay the bills and more is a nice feeling, but understand your limitations. The worst thing you can do is be a young artist that burns yourself out so fast that you don't enjoy creating anymore. Right now, I am super happy where I am and find fulfillment from the work I am making, so I'm focusing on that and seeing where it takes me. (However, I will say that I'm a fangirl of the fourth estate so one day being able to work with or for NPR would be super sick. Support your local public radio station!)" **Linnea Taylor, Multimedia Designer, School of Visual Arts, New York, New York (Class of 2016, BFA Design, School of Visual Arts, New York, New York)**

"To be honest, I was one of those people who had a plan and a vision for myself. Since graduating college, that path and journey has changed so much that my ultimate goal is happiness coupled with consistently providing hard work." **Masha Vainblat, Senior Digital Designer at Steven Madden, LTD, Long Island City, New York (Class of 2016, BFA Design, School of Visual Arts, New York, New York)**

"I try not to think too far ahead in life because it stresses me out a lot trying to curate my future when it's not really in my control. With that said, I would love to become a full time design instructor at a college like SVA, and hopefully climb my way up to be a creative director or senior designer of sorts, designing things that help humanity and sustain the world we live in." **Yejee Pae, Junior Designer, Communal Creative, New York, New York (Class of 2018, BFA Design, School of Visual Arts, New York, New York)**

Networking

While you're still in school, it's important to take advantage of networking opportunities to start building connections. Networking can occur at industry events, portfolio reviews, studio visits conferences, workshops, and any other gathering. The idea is simple—you walk up to a professional, introduce yourself, and get to know each other. You're not alone if the thought of talking to strangers makes you anxious. Networking can be daunting and intimidating, but here are some sample questions and conversation starters that you can use to feel confident working the crowd.

Sample networking questions:

Where do you work?
What do you do?
How long have you worked at [company]?
How do you like it there?
What kind of projects do you work on?
What's your favorite part of [company]?
How did you get hired at [company]?
What's the work environment like?
What's your day-to-day?

31

Some self-contradictory advice for the new designer
by Sean King, Senior Web Designer, PVH Corp

I have been making my living as a graphic designer since 1994. I've learned a lot along the way—often the hard way. Here are a few pieces of advice that I wish someone had told me when I was starting out. Design is full of contradictions, and this writing is no different: I will contradict myself with every piece of advice.

Note that I say *new* designer, not *young* designer. You don't have to be young to start in this field. Good designers are also always new, in that they are always trying to practice, to learn, to improve, to expand. I hope these thoughts help you as you embark on your design career.

Embrace the chaos!
Design is messy. Design is about exploration. Follow blind alleys, turn unexpected corners, backtrack, and return to earlier ideas. Your exploration can open clients' minds, changing their thinking, changing the project goal. Don't expect it to be straightforward, and don't expect to go home at five. It's all part of the job, enjoy it.

BUT

Be systematic
Creative doesn't have to mean disorganized. Don't make your job tougher by adding chaos to it. Record ideas when they occur to you. Date your sketches and keep them. Take notes. Use a file naming scheme. Back up your files. Use actions, use style sheets, use grids. Name your layers, keep editable versions of everything. Save and date all your PDFs. Keep a swipe file of ideas to turn to. Use your time well.

You learn design by designing
Reading a book on the guitar won't make you a musician: you need to practice. Design is the same way. You will only learn by practicing. Design for clients, design for friends, design for family, create your own projects. Design whenever you can.

BUT

Your education never ends
A degree is just the beginning, and you can only learn so much on your own. Read about design, see other designers present their work, watch them work if you can, watch tutorials, go to conferences, take classes. Take every opportunity to increase your knowledge and improve your skills. Seek experienced opinions and harsh critiques.

Become an authority
Learn all you can. Learn about theory and practice. Know how 4-color printing works, how inkjet printing works, how a camera works, how CSS works. Understand file formats and color theory. Become the person your colleagues can turn to for knowledge. Be helpful without being a snob, and you will become invaluable to your team.

BUT

Always ask questions
Don't ever be afraid to admit you don't know what someone is referring to. Ask what they mean, ask how it works. Take the print shop tour, watch the software demo. There is always more to learn, and technology and practices are always changing. Most people are very happy to share what they know with you.

"Yes, and. . ."
This is a guiding principle of improvisational comedy. Say yes to someone else's idea, then add to it. Designers don't need to get on stage without a script, but we do need to collaborate with others. Look for the good in another person's idea and build on it. Do this to make brainstorming productive and fun.

BUT

"Less is more"
Mies van der Rohe was talking about architecture when he said this, but it applies to all design. Your clients and bosses will often urge you to design a Swiss army knife. Try to design a scalpel instead. Communicate clearly and do away with anything that doesn't further your message.

Experiment
Play with conventions. Play with placement, with format, with color, with image, with type. Question every assumption. "That's the way we've always done it" isn't a good enough reason to keep doing it that way. You can surprise and delight by doing the unexpected.

BUT

Don't overthink it
Standards exist for a reason, because they usually work. Make it clear, make it legible, don't confuse your audience. Sometimes the business card works best at standard size, and sometimes the ad works best with the headline at the top and the logo in the lower right. Being different for its own sake won't help your work.

Design is awesome, so love it!

People working behind the counter at a fast food place have a right to be bored, designers do not. Our job is awesome, we are paid to make pictures. Even on a very bad day, we have a cooler job than 90% of the workforce. Remember this, and love it. And if you don't love it, do something else. There are far easier and more profitable professions out there. You should choose a career in design because you love it.

BUT

Don't be a doormat

You can love your work and still get paid. Beware of people who devalue design to get it free or fast. Don't do spec work, which includes creating new work for contests. Make sure you are paid fairly, and have contracts. If someone can't pay with money, maybe you can barter goods or services. If they don't want to pay you anything, then they probably don't value your hard work. Check Jessica Hische's shouldiworkforfree.com to help decide. (The answer is usually *no*.)

Don't worry about being unique, worry about being good.

Remember the old saying: "There is nothing new under the sun." No matter how brilliant the idea, someone else has had it before. So what? Make it new, make it fresh, make it awesome, and make it your own.

BUT

Don't steal

Don't copy other designers outright. It's lazy, it's lame, it sucks, it hurts your reputation and it could get you sued. You can take inspiration from other designers, build on their ideas, take them to new places, use them as starting points. Just don't transparently steal.

Ideas are everywhere, just look

We live in a designed world. If you live in a city, 90% of your surroundings are designed by people to serve a purpose for people. There is a wealth of design ideas and inspiration all around you, that most people tune out as background noise. Just open your eyes and look.

BUT

You have to refill the well

Creativity can be like a battery: it can run low, and it can give out completely. Recharge. Change your surroundings. Absorb great design work, great art, music, dance, fashion, film. Seek out the exceptional and the enjoyable. Don't just view passively: think about the creative decisions behind everything. It will revitalize your creativity.

Ideas are precious, nurture them

An idea, when it first pops into your head, can be like a baby bird in the nest. Give it time, shelter it, feed it. Don't subject it to harsh criticism before you've developed it. If its a good idea, it will fly soon enough. And even if it doesn't fly, it may be the seed for an even better idea later.

BUT

Ideas are easy, be ruthless with them

If the idea didn't fly, don't mourn it. It's not actually your baby. It didn't work, so it's not the right idea for the job. Move on to the next one. You've got a million more where that came from.

Find a mentor (or two)

When you find a friend with more experience than you, develop that friendship. Ask their opinion, ask their advice. The help they can give you with your design work, your career, and workplace politics is invaluable.

BUT

You are your own best advocate

No one will be as concerned for your career as you are. If things aren't right in your workplace, with your client, with your salary or title, speak up. And if that doesn't change things, look for a better opportunity. No one else will do it for you.

Be shameless about self-promotion

Share your work with the world. Blog, tweet, publish, build an awesome web portfolio. Enter your work in competitions. Join professional organizations and go to their events. Meet people and don't be shy about handing out your business card. Potential clients and employers expect to find your work online. Most opportunities arise through personal relationships. Ensure that both these things can happen easily.

BUT

Don't be pushy

Let people know who you are and what you can do, but be a genuine person. Be someone who is good to work with and people will want to work with you. If your work shines, there is no need to be a used-car salesman. Put your talent out there and let it speak for itself.

Be awesome

Push yourself and push your work. Don't settle for OK, or for good enough. Don't even settle for great. Aim for awesome and keep pushing until you get there. Be your own harshest critic, and don't let yourself off the hook. Great designers don't win a talent lottery, they work hard on every job.

BUT

You don't have to be a superstar

There are many steps between famous and failure. You don't have to be famous to be a good designer, and you don't need to be the greatest to have a good career. Look at movie credits: hundreds of people are in involved in a film. The director and the actors can't do it by themselves, and neither can superstar designers. They all have help behind the scenes. There is a lot of work out there if you are talented, disciplined, and pleasant to work with.

Creating a great portfolio

3

You have great work that you're proud to get out there, how do you put it all together to impress a hiring manager or a creative director? In this chapter, we'll go over types of portfolios, how to get feedback on your work, and advice on what hiring managers look for in a portfolio.

When creating a portfolio, keep in mind these 5 top tips:

- Curate your work

- Go for variety

- Invest in photography

- Write about your work

- Keep it current

Types of portfolios

Physical print portfolios

Printed portfolio books are slowly being phased out by digital books. However, if your work is mainly print and you're looking for a way to showcase your printed work, a strong custom printed portfolio can demonstrate attention to detail and passion for print. The key is not duplicating your website, but taking advantage of every detail such as paper selection, binding, size, and every inch of the page.

Printed portfolio books can easily cost you from $50 to even over $1,000 for a custom made book. While there's no need to go into massive debt to get the best custom book created with all the bells and whistles, you do need to choose the details of your printed book to align with your personal branding and style.

Less is more. The basic rule of the printed portfolio is that your work should be the memorable visual in the portfolio, all the details of the book should enhance the work, not distract from it. Are the pages big enough to showcase the work? Are the images sharp and not pixelated? Does the binding allow the pages to turn easily with one hand, or do they get stuck? Does the book allow you to shuffle around pages and update the book easily?

Supplement with digital. In addition to bringing your printed book, your website is a good supplement to show in an interview in case you'd like to share personal projects not included in your printed book.

Most creative directors will appreciate seeing a designer's personal work. It helps them get to know you as a designer, and as a person.

Online portfolios

A strong, professional, and accessible portfolio is the most important piece to presenting your best work to a potential employer. Digital portfolios have become a standard practice among applicants.

An online portfolio is open 24/7/365. It's always live to showcase who you are as a designer.

Mobile friendly. In today's mobile driven environment, you must have a portfolio that is 100% mobile friendly. Most recruiters and creative directors will come in contact with your work through a link, and there is a high chance that they'll visit your portfolio on their phones. Make sure your portfolio is accessible on mobile.

Choose your platform. To set up your portfolio, buy a personalized domain name, invest in a hosting/platform provider, and design your site. There are many different platforms for creating bespoke design portfolios. The most popular platforms are:

- Squarespace
- Semplice Labs
- Cargo
- WIX

Alternatively, consider developing your website yourself, or ask a tech-savvy friend to help you set up your website. Remember to share credit, if you do.

Tip corner: Advice from recent graduates

Portfolio advice

What advice would you give to students on how to build a strong portfolio?

"Quality over quantity! If I'm going through a portfolio and see even one project that is weak (even if the rest of the work is great), I am immediately turned off. And if you feel you don't have enough work that you're proud of, that's where side projects and self-initiated work comes in. I also think presentation of your work makes a huge difference and can really elevate a portfolio to another level. For example, if you have a branding project, show mock-ups of the brand in an interesting environment." **Anna Rising, Designer & Illustrator, Oslo, Norway (Class of 2015, BFA Graphic Design, University of the Arts in Philadelphia, Pennsylvania)**

"Don't be afraid to scrap everything and start over. Often times restarting a project from the very foundation helps in getting a better idea of where things might have gone wrong and could be improved. Also do lots of research! Nothing worse than seeing something very similar to your work on the internet, though it happens so often 'unintentionally'. (But then again—does originality even exist? Food for thought.)" **Ein Jung, Product Designer, Bunch, New York, New York (Class of 2018, BFA Advertising and Design, School of Visual Arts, New York, New York)**

"On a macro level, show your best work with beautiful visual images. On a micro level, display and talk about processes when it's appropriate—most people probably won't read it, but it's there for those that care. Also, don't be boring when talking about yourself in your portfolio—don't be afraid to show personality." **Hieu Tran, Product Designer, OpenSpace, San Francisco, California (Class of 2016, MFA Graphic Design, Maryland Institute College of Art, Baltimore, Maryland)**

"Only show your best work that you are passionate about. Don't showcase work in your portfolio that you don't want to be hired to do professionally. The presentation of your work, both visually and how you talk about it, is part of the design." **Jason Fujikuni, Art Director, Brand Identity** *The New York Times*, **New York, New York (Class of 2017, BFA Graphic Design, Rhode Island School of Design, Providence, Rhode Island)**

"My advice to students trying to build their portfolio would be to curate yourself. Not everything you make is going to be amazing, use your portfolio for those things that are. Don't have enough projects? Then make some stuff. Don't let your class projects dictate your portfolio, find things that inspire you and think of how to make a project out of it. Don't be discouraged by other people's work, you can only do what you do, so don't worry about what everyone else is doing. I would also say try to make projects that are outside of what you know. For example, I branded a 90's rap bakery, something I knew nothing about, but you best believe I listened to 90s rap for a whole week, watched music videos, and movies just so I could have a grasp on the content and it's one of my favorite projects. Sometimes our best work comes from a fresh perspective." **Julia Whitley, Graphic Designer, Barkley, Kansas City, Missouri (Class of 2017, BFA Graphic Design, Oklahoma State University, Stillwater, Oklahoma)**

"Take initiatives and invest some time and energy in the 'passion projects.' You would be able to talk about these projects with more excitement and detail. My opinion is that a strong portfolio is one that expresses who you are as a designer. While most skills can be acquired or improved on the job, but a unique perspective is something that's impossible to teach." **June Shin, Type Designer, Occupant Fonts/Morisawa USA, Providence, Rhode Island (Class of 2017, MFA Graphic Design, Rhode Island School of Design, Providence, Rhode Island)**

37

Tip corner: Advice from recent graduates

"Starting a portfolio, especially if there's a deadline, is all about asset management—trust me, it saves a lot of time. When wrapping up a project, imagine how you'd like to see that work live in whatever space you decide for it. Whether it's printed, digital or a website, create assets to show the process, mock-ups for the finished pieces, or whatever else you would like to highlight and have those finished and saved along with the rest of the work. When it comes time to put everything together, you are then able to have all the content you could need on hand and place it as you see fit and focus on the portfolio presentation, instead of taking precious time to create more content to fill space or construct storylines of projects. When you start with all your assets, you're able to simply place the content, curate it faster, and focusing on presenting it in the best way possible." **Linnea Taylor, Multimedia Designer, School of Visual Arts, New York, New York (Class of 2016, BFA Design, School of Visual Arts, New York, New York)**

"Sometimes uncertainty is okay as long as you have your inner voice guiding you. If there is a mentor who cares enough to sit down and review your work or help you to develop your concept, take advantage of that. Also, don't forget to step back and breathe to get a better idea of a full picture." **Masha Vainblat, Senior Digital Designer at Steven Madden, LTD, Long Island City, New York (Class of 2016, BFA Design, School of Visual Arts, New York, New York)**

"Establish a system that works for you. Create a timeline, and a deadline for yourself that is before your actual portfolio due date so that you have a little wiggle room. Set up weekly or biweekly deadlines within your timeline that you must keep so that you are not pulling a 4 day overnight to finish your last (and most important) project of the semester." **Yejee Pae, Junior Designer, Communal Creative, New York, New York (Class of 2018, BFA Design, School of Visual Arts, New York, New York)**

What are your most reliable and/or unlikely sources of inspiration?

"Social Media (Instagram, Behance, Dribbble)

Other designers (I usually find them on sites like WorkingNotWorking, CreativeMornings or through awards like the Art Directors Club 'Young Guns' awards)

Podcasts (Design Matters, Meet The Creatives)

Design blogs (Mindsparkle Mag, It's Nice That, The Dieline)

Traveling to new cities and meeting new people "

Anna Rising, Designer & Illustrator, Oslo, Norway (Class of 2015, BFA Graphic Design, University of the Arts in Philadelphia, Pennsylvania)

"I try to read as much as I can, about subjects totally unrelated to design or art. If often gives the occupied mind some much needed breathing room for new ideas. I also find talking to other creatives super inspiring. But other than that, few of my online sources include:

visuelle.co.uk

itsnicethat.com

identitydesigned.com

Few offline sources include:

Printed Matter

McNally Jackson Independant Books

Standard Manuel

Assouline"

Ein Jung, Product Designer, Bunch, New York, New York (Class of 2018, BFA Advertising and Design, School of Visual Arts, New York, New York)

"Medium articles

Restaurant menus (99% of the time I want to redesign them)

Street murals

Mental breaks

Thrift stores"

Hieu Tran, Product Designer, OpenSpace, San Francisco, California (Class of 2016, MFA Graphic Design, Maryland Institute College of Art, Baltimore, Maryland)

"Nature

Bodies of water

Sculpture & furniture design

Independent bookstores

Museums

Graphic novels & artists books

Bible"

Jason Fujikuni, Art Director, Brand Identity *The New York Times*, **New York, New York (Class of 2017, BFA Graphic Design, Rhode Island School of Design, Providence, Rhode Island)**

"Walks in my neighborhood

Documentaries, recently 'Ugly Delicious' on Netflix. I work with a lot of food, so this show has been super inspiring.

A lot of Pinterest (shamefully)

Instagram: potters, pie makers, muralists, wood workers

@rmalindesign

@karinpfeiffboschek

@tortus

@stefankunz

New York Times Magazine"

Julia Whitley, Graphic Designer, Barkley, Kansas City, Missouri (Class of 2017, BFA Graphic Design, Oklahoma State University, Stillwater, Oklahoma)

"Literature

The streets (my quotidian surroundings)

Conversations (with anyone, not just other designers)

History"

June Shin, Type Designer, Occupant Fonts/Morisawa USA, Providence, Rhode Island (Class of 2017, MFA Graphic Design, Rhode Island School of Design, Providence, Rhode Island)

"MEMES

designspiration.net

stumbleupon.com"

Masha Vainblat, Senior Digital Designer at Steven Madden, LTD, Long Island City, New York (Class of 2016, BFA Design, School of Visual Arts, New York, New York)

"Itsnicethat.com

Mindsparklemag.com

Siteinspire.com

Visuelle.co.uk"

Yejee Pae, Junior Designer, Communal Creative, New York, New York (Class of 2018, BFA Design, School of Visual Arts, New York, New York)

Portfolio examples

The portfolio examples shown here are from Linnea Taylor, Ein Jung, Jason Fujikuni, and Masha Vainblat.

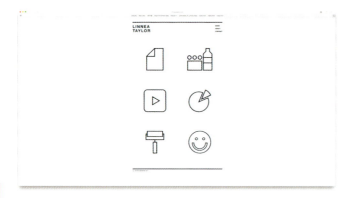 

Linnea Taylor

Ein Jung

 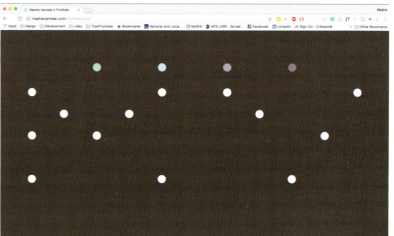

Jason Fujikuni

Masha Vainblat

Top 5 tips for creating a portfolio
by Rietje Becker, Creative Director at Soulsight

Tip 1: You are your own brand

Show off your knowledge of branding by creating your own personal logo and visual system. Think about what makes you different than other designers, and use this as a brief to create a logo, type treatment, color palette, etc., that communicates your unique abilities. Apply this design to your portfolio, resume, website, process book, and other promotional materials. Dedicate the same time and passion to creating your personal brand that you would to any school project. This is the first thing people will see, so it should make a good impression. Your brand should be subtle in its placement and prominence so that it will not distract from the projects you are sharing.

Tip 2: Layout and format

You will need several portfolio formats, but the most important is your portfolio website. This will likely be the first stop for potential employers and will determine whether they call you in for an interview. It should be branded using your personal brand, typeface, etc. Unless you are a programmer who would like to show off a custom created site, using templated sites like squarespace.com is useful. The projects should be easy to navigate and in a format that's adaptable to multiple devices, like tablets or phones. Check that emails and phone numbers are accurate.

You should have a second version of your portfolio to be used for your interviews. It should utilize a grid, consistent type style, size. and usage. The layout should work well for screen and print. Cater the mix of projects to the interests of the agency with whom you are meeting. Don't show more than 8–10 projects. Each one should have multiple pages that show the depth of your idea.

Do a practice interview and see how long it takes you to go through your projects. Memorize a few things to say about each page. Make sure you can go through your presentation quickly (about 15 minutes) since most interviewers are limited in time. If you have a more patient interviewer you can always add more detail. Adjust the quantity of work accordingly.

Portfolios today do not need to be print-based, although having a printed version may be requested or needed for portfolio shows. When a printed book is needed, consider working with a local printer to produce it. Photo book printers can work, too. Do some research to see what places offer more creative flexibility. While a photo book printer will not give you much control over color, it will give you a nicely finished book relatively inexpensively.

Tip 3: Mind your details

Any information you share, on your website, in your portfolio, leave-behind, or resume, should be checked for spelling and grammar.

If possible, get a photographer or friend who knows photography to take some beauty shots of your work. Keep things simple in your staging. Not too much propping, keep the focus on your work. If you do not have acceptable photography use renderings instead. Sites like livesurface.com or shutterstock.com can provide images to use at a low cost.

Tip 4: DOs and DON'Ts

Do consider having sharing some of your early design options. This will show the viewer the true range of your exploration. Exploratory is not needed for all work.

Do make sure your design style varies from one project to the next. This will show employers that you are able to design for different design challenges and projects.

Do list information about the purpose of each of your projects. Viewers should be able to navigate your work, without you there to explain them.

When including projects from internships or previous jobs do ensure that there is no work that can't be shown publicly. Many companies have confidentiality agreements with their clients, and featuring work you did for them in your portfolio could get the agency fired as a client, and you in legal trouble.

Don't include work you don't like. People will judge you by your strongest and weakest project.

Don't include a type of project you are not interested in working on in the future. People will hire you based on the work they see.

People often bring printed samples from internships or previous jobs. Don't show these unless asked. Just because they are 'real' does not mean they are great examples of your work.

Tip 5: More than a portfolio

Often employers will ask about your creative process, consider creating a separate presentation where you take one of your strongest projects and show in greater detail how you went from sketch to final execution.

Have multiple printed resumes ready at your interview, this should list relevant design experience like internships, but does not need to include previous non-design related jobs.

Few places require a cover letter, but prepare a template, just in case. If needed, cater the content of the letter to the company, their interests, and the position listed.

Create a promotional card or booklet, something that will help people remember your best projects. This can be shared prior to interviews, as a leave-behind at portfolio shows, or at your interview in the hope that they will hang on to it, and remember you as they make their staffing decisions.

"About" page examples

Your portfolio's "About" page
is a chance for you to introduce
yourself and share a little of your
personality. It's also best practice
to include a link to your resume
and contact information.

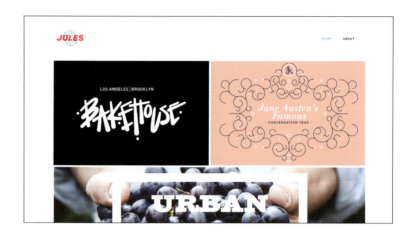

42

Julia Whitley's "About"
page has a great balance of
personality (i.e., "Likes cats
and striped shirts" in the left
rail), a brief summary about
herself, a link to a PDF of her
resume, social media links, and
contact information.

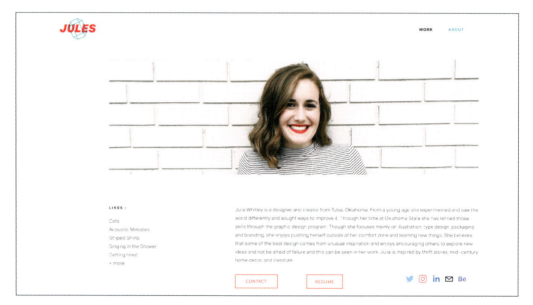

Linnea Taylor

How to write about your work

Your portfolio should include finished design work, along with your design process. Potential employers want to know how you arrived at a particular solution, so consider documenting your work and writing about your design process.

For each project, you'll want to create a project brief—a story of what problem you were trying to solve and how you arrived at the solution.

Your design brief might look something like the diagram on the right.

Key elements of a design brief:

- Define the problem and state the purpose of the work
- Define who the work is for (target audience)
- Articulate the solution: key messages/information, how it's different from the competition

[Images of the project, as a single configuration]

Project Title: (write the title of this project)
Challenge: (describe the project, and its challenge)
Solution: (describe how you solved the problem)

43

PEEK

TYPOGRAPHY : DIGITAL PUBLICATION

04

Each project in Hiue Tran's portfolio uses consistent typographic hierarchy to title each piece, along with a brief description and bold visuals.

Peek is a tablet story aggregator that gives its readers a glimpse into the lives of many unique and talented individuals. The app seeks to gather its stories mostly from independent magazine websites such as Hello Mr., Kinfolk, Jocks & Nerds, and The Gentlewoman. Peek organizes its content in one of the following three forms: long read profiles, photo essays, and interviews.

How to photograph your work

Professional quality photographs of your work are a must, whether you're creating a physical or a digital portfolio. You're presenting yourself and your work online, so give potential employers a strong first impression of your craft.

Don't stress if you don't have a top-of-the-line camera or if you're not the most skilled photographer. You can rely on your skills in composition and art direction to set up your shots and use basic camera equipment to get great results.

Anna Rising's personal project, Kanvas. "All packaging was printed on Cardstock at my local FedEx location and assembled by myself or placed on products that I found in my home (such as the nail polish and bubble bath). All product photography was shot on a Cannon T3 in a makeshift photo studio I made in my home."

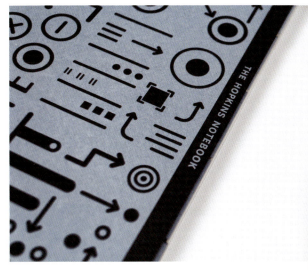

Shoot your print projects at an angle to create dynamic compositions.

Left: Hieu Tran "The Hopkins Notebook,"
Below: Julia Whitley, "The Urban Farm."

Portfolio photography tips

Art direct your shoot. You're the client and the art director in your shoot. Choose the background, props, and composition that best highlights your work.

When in doubt, keep it simple. You don't want to go overboard with a cluttered background.

Photograph your pieces individually.

Try to fill the camera frame with your work.

If you are able to use professional equipment, that's an added bonus! You may wish to consider using a DSLR camera for projects that have a physical quality to them, such as special printing techniques, production, or fabrication.

Adjust the white balance settings on your camera. If possible, shoot your work in a consistent location with consistent lighting. For example, if you're shooting indoors, block other light sources, and use two sources of light.

Consider investing in a backdrop, daylights, and shop lights for a home setup that you can re-use later in your career whenever you add more work to your portfolio.

Try it again and again.

Most importantly, have patience. Try different compositions, different camera settings, or adjust the light until you're happy with the result. Photograph your work again if you're not getting perfect images. Ask a friend to help, if necessary.

How to present your work

You've spent countless nights perfecting your photography, descriptions, and portfolio pieces. Once you're confident in your portfolio being ready, it's time to get eyes on your work and solicit feedback. Reaching out to your personal and professional network is a great way to get your portfolio seen and gather quick feedback on what you can improve. When asking people to check out your site, consider asking for a critique. Many creatives enjoy providing constructive feedback on others' work.

46

Dos and don'ts of using social media to ask for a portfolio critique:

Do: Connect directly with the person you're messaging or DMing, ask for feedback and action steps.

Do: Personalize your DM to each person you're reaching out to.

Do: Include your portfolio link everywhere (your email signature, social media presence, business card, etc.).

Don't: Use generic messages to everyone, such as "Big news! My portfolio is here. Check out [url]."

Don't: Forget to say thank you and connect with the person on other social media channels, such as LinkedIn.

Example DM:

Hi [Designer], I saw your company recently launched [specific campaign], congratulations! I'd love to work at [Company]and wanted to share my updated portfolio with you for feedback and a critique. Let me know your thoughts on my portfolio, [url].

Dos and don'ts of emailing a request for a portfolio critique:

Do: Be direct with your request, giving the person a description of exactly the type of feedback you're looking for and when you'd like to receive it.

Do: Expect to send follow-up emails if you haven't heard back.

Do: Send a thank you note immediately after receiving feedback.

Do: Send an update when you've reflected on the feedback and ask the person to share your updated portfolio with their network.

Don't: Get frustrated if you don't hear back. Send a follow-up!

Don't: Limit yourself to professionals in the creative field. Consider non-creatives from your professional network. For example, a critique and a share from a CEO of a company you've done freelance work for could be more valuable than a designer you're loosely connected to on social media.

Example Email:

Hi [Name],

I recently finished updating my portfolio and wanted to get some feedback on it before starting my job search in [industry]. One thing I was wondering about is [describe exactly what feedback you're looking for]. Could you please review my portfolio and share your feedback by [date]? I'd love to get your honest opinion and advice. My portfolio url is [url].

Thank you,

[Your Name]

Ask the professionals:
What do creative directors look for in a portfolio?

Learn what top creative directors look for when they're hiring.

What do you look for in a portfolio when you're hiring?

"I look for a broad spectrum of experience. It's important for candidates to understand how to apply design across all platforms. This includes print and web, branding, signage, whatever. I also look for work that is smart and has meaning. Is the design solution clear? Does it communicate what it needs to? Bonus points for that special something that makes you stand out." **Lara McCormick, Freelance Creative Director, San Francisco, California**

"I look for smart thinking and great craft. I like to see people who can solve a range of problems that are outside their own comfort zone. I like to see they have complete thoughts and depth in problem solving. I also love the rare find of someone who thinks differently or comes from an out of the way or unconventional place. Sometimes they don't fit the mold or pedigree, of a typical creative, but bring something new to the table in how to create or solve problems." **Kris Kiger, Executive Vice President, Executive Creative Director, Design, R/GA, New York, New York**

"Usability of your website is key. Doesn't need to be fancy, either. For individual pieces of work, I want to understand the process and not just the outcome. What insight did you have about the consumer of your work, if any? And what would you do different next time, or how would you evolve what you've done? That said, like any designer, the pretty pictures will get me every time, so no need to write a novel." **Emily Wengert, Group Vice President, User Experience, Huge, Brooklyn, New York**

"It's nice to see an actual physical portfolio, or at least a few pieces that I can hold in my hands. I've come to accept viewing projects on an iPad Pro, but am not fond of looking at work on a laptop or having someone point me to their website. It's good to see projects that mean something to the designer as well as a few pieces that are grounded in reality—it's hard to just see experimental work. I need to know that the candidate is capable of doing real stuff, too.

Ultimately, it's about the person on the other side of the desk. Is this someone who might fit comfortably into the group? Someone I'd feel good about teaching and working closely with? Is there a whiff of quirky or is that a whiff of crazy? It's all grist for the mill." **Gail Anderson, Chair, BFA Design and BFA Advertising, Creative Director, Visual Arts Press, School of Visual Arts, New York, New York**

"In-house teams are usually small, and need to be nimble in order to adapt to quick shifts in organization priorities. Because of that, a great attitude, flexibility to create work across different mediums, and strong craft are what I look for." **Ida Woldemichael, Associate Creative Director, Wide Eye, Washington D.C.**

"Two things: I always look for something that I would love to have done. Something I've never seen. And then I pay close attention to side projects. I've hired a lot of people with medium portfolios but with incredible side projects." **Fred Saldanha, Global Chief Creative Officer, VMLY&R, New York, New York**

"A clear problem the design is working to solve.

Sharp, refined, and clean visuals. No unnecessary elements or anything that detracts from the problem you're solving.

A unique twist or unexpected delight that makes the design product memorable." **Ryan Scott Tandy, Product Design Manager, Instagram, San Francisco, California**

Portfolio clinic

This section features samples from young designers' portfolios accompanied by design experts' evaluation and advice, as well as advice to the reader on what works in the portfolio and areas for improvement. The range of featured portfolios (both print and digital) gives a full breadth of work and helpful evaluation and commentary by the design luminaries. Each portfolio review in this section is accompanied by tip boxes, colophons of fonts used, production details, vendors, special printing techniques used, software/tools used to build the digital prototypes, etc., to help the reader use the portfolios as models and reference points for their own pursuits.

Portfolio Spotlight on. . .

48

Anna Rising

Rosemary

Typeface Design

Rosemary is a stencil display typeface inspired by organic shapes and forms and developed at the University of the Arts under the instruction of Berton Hasebe. The type specimen book was a concept that was mocked up in Photoshop.

Software used: RoboFont, Adobe Photoshop

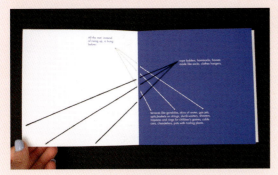

Invisible Cities

Print

A series of booklets based around three sections in Italo Calvino's *Invisible Cities*. Made for my Advanced Typography class at University of the Arts under the instruction of Debra Drodvillo. Printed at the University of the Arts Print Services lab. The booklets were printed using an InkJet printer to retain the vibrant colors.

Software used: Adobe Indesign, Photoshop, and Illustrator

Tools used: Thread (I sewed thread into the pages of the *Chloe* book), Vellum (some pages of *Octavia* were printed separately on Vellum)

Fonts used: Futura. All calligraphy and lettering was hand-drawn by myself and scanned into Photoshop.

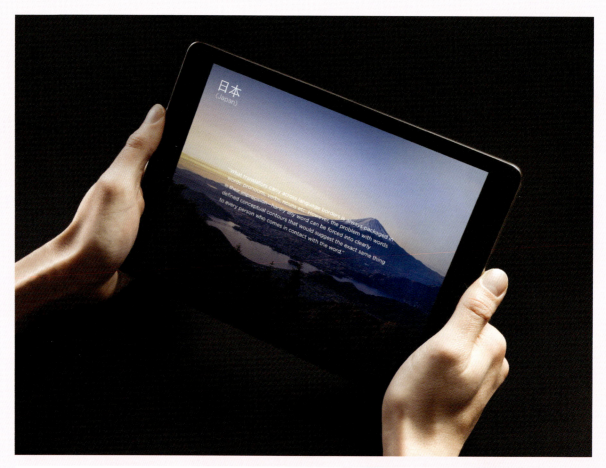

The Other Side

Digital

The Other Side is an interactive iPad application that explores translation and language through untranslatable words. Made for my senior degree project at the University of the Arts under the instruction of Jan Almquist. This app was fully functional on an iPad: https://vimeo.com/147798231.

Software used: Origami Studio, Adobe Photoshop and Illustrator, Adobe After Effects

you're watching
Rainier Twenty Ten

next
Mt. McKinley Climb *(live)*

FEARLESS

CURRENT

CRUX

Branding and motion graphics

CRUX Television is a mountaineering cable channel concept that shows adventure as it happens. Crux Television features live climbing treks from all types of climbers in all types of conditions. Made during my senior year at University of the Arts under the instruction of Debra Drodvillo.

Software used: Adobe AfterEffects, Photoshop, and Illustrator. Video Footage was pulled from Vimeo.

Fonts used: Brooklyn (display),

Motion Graphics: https://vimeo.com/126828133, https://vimeo.com/126827616, https://vimeo.com/126750048, https://vimeo.com/127162791

Praxis

Event Branding

Praxis was the 2015 graphic design senior show at the University of the Arts in Philadelphia, Pennsylvania. Praxis showcased the graduating senior's thesis projects and other selected works. I was a part of the branding and web team and worked with Greg Falconi, John Brown, Frederick Lee, and Min Kyong Kim to conceptualize and create the brand, assets, and website.

Everything was printed at the University of the Arts Print Services lab.

Software used: Adobe Photoshop and Illustrator

Fonts used: Avenir

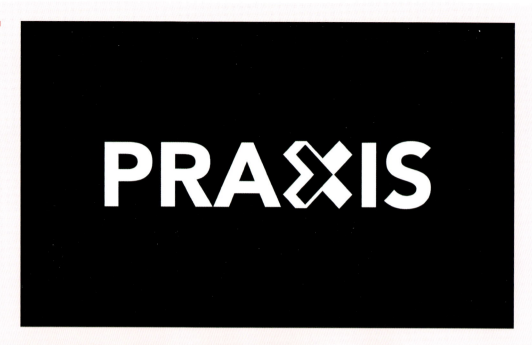

52

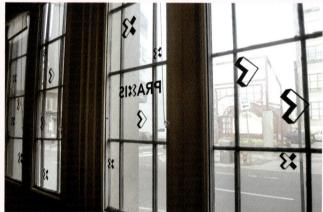

Related

UI/UX

Related is a co-collaborative website that explores family resemblance among siblings. The entire site was coded by me using HTML, CSS, and jQuery. Made during my senior year at the University of the Arts under the instruction of Debra Drodvillo.

Software used: BBEdit, Adobe Illustrator, Photoshop

Note: my favorite part of this project was the video I made that describes the project, that can be found here: https://vimeo.com/115036649. Video was made using Adobe AfterEffects.

Personal projects

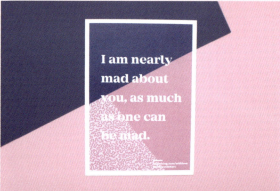

To _____, With Love.

Print and digital

A personal project devoted to spreading love around the world. 2016 was a rough year. To combat all the hate around the world, I sent love letters to friends and strangers because—let's face it— we could all use a little extra love. Through a website, users can submit their address for a free postcard. I sent over 100 postcards to people in over 5 different countries (and counting!). All postcards were printed double-sided and trimmed at Paper Presentation in New York City. All quotes and excerpts were pulled from various online sources. This project was entirely self-directed.

Software used: Adobe Illustrator and InDesign

54

Within branded packaging, the beauty category is among the most clichéd. And within this, branded packaging for kids is the worst.

Kanvas is a brand concept aimed at breaking down gender stereotypes and beauty stigmas from the roots: with kids. Kanvas promotes gender neutral products that promote self-expression, originality and creativity.

Boys don't wear nail polish.

Even now in 2016, a time where generations are becoming more and more accepting, there is still a negative stigma when it comes to boys wearing nail polish. But why is this? When it comes down to it, nail polish is just paint for your fingers. Paint and color are not limited to one gender, so why is nail polish? It's just another form of self-expression, after all.

This idea is the basis of Kanvas.

Kanvas

Branding and packaging

Kanvas is a brand and packaging concept created for the 2016 Design Bridge D&AD New Blood Brief. This project was entirely self-directed.

The Brief: Within branded packaging, the beauty category is among the most clichéd. Why do men's personal care products look like power tools, whilst women's remain delicate and ultra feminine? The world has moved on. Create a new-to-world, accessible, mass-market beauty brand that breaks established category codes. Your brand should be a response to some of the issues with which modern, post-demographic consumers identify: gender stereotypes, healthy body image, environmental concerns, or any other issues you feel are relevant to users of beauty products today.

All packaging was printed on Cardstock at my local FedEx location and assembled by myself or placed on products that I found in my home (such as the nail polish and bubble bath). All product photography was shot on a Cannon T3 in a makeshift photo studio I made in my home.

Software used: Adobe Illustrator and Photoshop

Portfolio Critique by Julia Zeltser
Creative Director & Partner, Hyperakt
Brooklyn, New York

What is your overall impression of this portfolio? What do you like and why?

"Anna has some exciting work in her portfolio. One of the elements I look for in student work is a strong documentation skill as well as diversity of execution. I can't say enough about how important those two elements are. Strong photography, mock ups, and the overall presentation of the work speaks of design confidence, care, and maturity. Beautiful documentation in itself can make the original work more elevated than the actual end product. And luckily, I see not only a lot of great work, but also strong documentation in Anna's portfolio.

Take 'Kanvas' project, for example, the brand is wonderfully bright, playful, energetic—in line with what parents (the intended audience) need to see in the product. I like the blobs of paint swarming around each other as one set of texture as well as an added textured lines/blobs to build a bit more depth. The textured blobs are used on a solid color background of a Temporary Hair Color Blue tube to signal a specific product. The logo anchors it all together. Strong design overall.

In 'With Love' project you'll find an example of beautiful documentation. The design of the postcards calls for various angles, and those angles are mimicked in the documentation. When looking at the postcard your eye travels well beyond, making the experience of viewing Anna's work a great joy.

When I review student portfolios, it takes a split of a second to form a decision on whether the designer is strong. The work that always stands out is when a student can show they make lots out of nothing, make design look fun or sophisticated, and document it perfectly. Not an easy task, but Anna's got it!"

What advice would you give on this portfolio for areas of improvement?

"Over the years I've seen various brands come to life in physical environments with popular applications such as billboards, T-shirts, stationery, and buttons. All that is happening in a very controlled surrounding with a product that won't significantly change with a user's interaction. However, the most difficult task for a brand designer is to show how the brand lives on the web. Anna's work shows a few subdued web applications like 'The Other Side.' But it would be interesting to see how a heavily branded product such as 'Kanvas' shapes online. Would there be as much color, or shapes, or textures? How will animation or video play a role?

I highly recommend for any designer to flex their muscles in a medium their work might appear in. Undoubtedly, it took years to polish your branding skills so why should anyone expect the same level of slickness in UX? The reality of our times is that we all have to have a flexible design arsenal—branding, retouching, UX, and a little code to name a few. The additional web mock up work is only a minor portion of the project but together they all paint a much stronger picture of you as a diverse, capable, and today's designer. One more push and keep up the good work!"

56

Portfolio Spotlight on. . .

Ein Jung

Bengala

Bengala is a natural fabric mud-dye made from the Earth. Inspired by the earthy qualities of the dyes' colors, the visual identity of the brand focuses on the colors themselves and the Japanese heritage it holds.

Fonts used: Clone Rounded Latin, Faircy New, Yuanti Bold

Software used: Adobe Photoshop and Illustrator

Blade Runner

A DVD package designed for the iconic sci-fi film, *Blade Runner*. The iconic movie is littered with stunning visuals—especially that of lighting design. Inspired by the colorful neon lights of the movie, this special edition package is an homage to *Blade Runner*'s significance in the sci-fi genre.

Fonts used: Beon, Elevate, Flottflott, Lakesight, Las Enter, Neon, Neonic, Neons, Rubber, Typo Round, Warnes

Software used: Adobe Photoshop, Illustrator, and InDesign.

Dot

Seeing that periods become a bigger struggle for women who are homeless, Dot was designed to make a positive impact on the lives of every women who decides to use it. It is a simple app that can be used to track and record your menstrual cycle—and help out homeless women with theirs.

Fonts used: Freight Display Pro, DIN alternate

Software used: Sketch and Adobe Illustrator and Photoshop

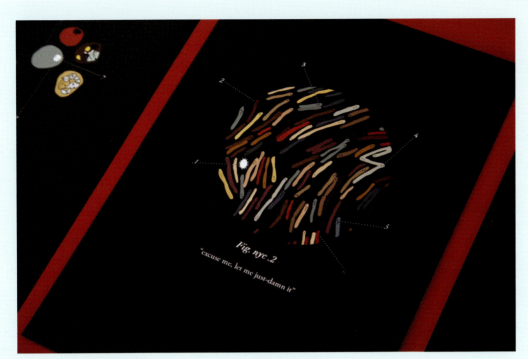

Fig. NYC

A series of postcard's for the big, pulsating organism: New York City. Drawing inspiration from the microscopic view of cells, this series of postcards illustrates the various sentiments one experiences while roaming around the city.

Fonts used: Didot, Garamond

Software used: Adobe Illustrator and Photoshop

Layered

A collection of five hand-bound books compiling a year's worth of work. Each book encompasses a variety of work, ranging from advertisements to posters. This portfolio compilation received a 5 out of 5 in the end of year department reviews.

Software used: Printed with Epson R2000, hand-bound (coptic stitch and Japanese stab binding tortoise stitch), box crafted by Celine Lombardi

Look. Book.

Playing with color and composition, this hand-bound look book explores the congruent hues of my wardrobe and bookshelf. A collaborative project with a photographer who helped set up the shoot and photograph myself.

Fonts used: Bressay, Apercu

Software used: Adobe Photoshop and InDesign; printed with Epson R2000 and hand-bound (coptic stich)

Museum of Stress

An interactive experience that embodies the spicy, stress-relieving qualities of Sriracha hot sauce. In coming up with the concept, the various illustrations were created to convey the gist of the exhibition.

Software used: Adobe Illustrator

TIEDY

Ties lined with microfiber
cloth for your glasses.

Tiedy

Look Sharp, See Sharper—neckties
lined with microfiber cloth to clean
your glasses. A brand new kind
of ties branded, prototyped, and
photographed by me. Tiedy is a multidisciplinary project in the workings of
becoming a reality.

Fonts used: Kazmann Sans, Archer
Pro Book

Software used: Adobe Photoshop and
Illustrator and Sketch

Zine: 5

The first step was to create a 100 typographic layouts using 5 typefaces. In choosing a dozen best compositions, this zine was created in celebration of Massimo Vignelli's famous five essential typefaces.

Fonts used: Bodoni, Futura, Helvetica, Times New Roman, Century

Software used: Adobe Illustrator and InDesign; printed with Epson R2000 and hand-bound

Portfolio Critique by Fred Saldanha
Executive Creative Director, Arnold Worldwide
Boston, Massachusetts

What is your overall impression of this portfolio? What do you like and why?

"I love to see insightful, inspiring and purposeful work. Ein Jung showed a little of that in her portfolio. I like the variety of her work, the care of the craft, the refinement of some projects. I feel there's still a lot of room to develop, but the potential is there.

My favorite piece is Tiedy. The project as a whole is smart, fun and useful."

What advice would you give on this portfolio for areas of improvement?

"I would tell Ein to dare more. Try new things. To invent. Get out of her comfort zone. Some projects seem like a continuation of the previous project. Every student portfolio has to somehow provoke the status quo. To show that a new generation is coming with new ideas, new ways of interacting with people and seeing the world."

Portfolio Spotlight on. . .

Hieu Tran

Circuit Cities

Circuit Cities is a conceptual design project where we were asked to develop an alter ego that amplifies, undermines, or rediscovers an element of ourselves. Theodore Watson, a former computer engineer, currently works as an architect and urban planner. His years of working in the engineering industry inspired his vision to create fictional cities using his design knowledge of circuit boards.

Software used: sketchfab.com to render 3D files, Adobe Illustrator and InDesign, Rhino 3D

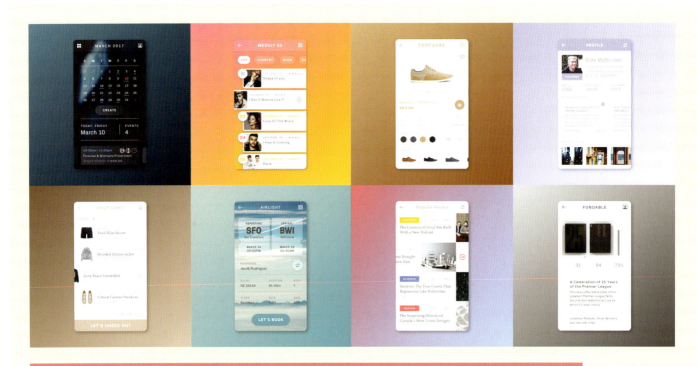

Daily UI challenge

In an attempt to better myself as an UI/UX designer, I designed an interface each day for 45 days on various subjects of my interest.

Software used: PX Grotesk, Platform, Apercu, Fayon, Relative, Feijoa, GT Pressura, Formular, Sketch App

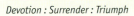

Devotion : Surrender : Triumph

Devotion : Surrender : Triumph is a project where I attempted to answer the question, "How can we give new meanings to patterns by using them in a new context through a process of deconstruction to reconstruction?" I was particularly interested in exploring the different ways I could transform a two-dimensional drawing and turn it into a three-dimensional object.

Software used: Laser Etching and Cutting, Adobe Illustrator, Rhino 3D

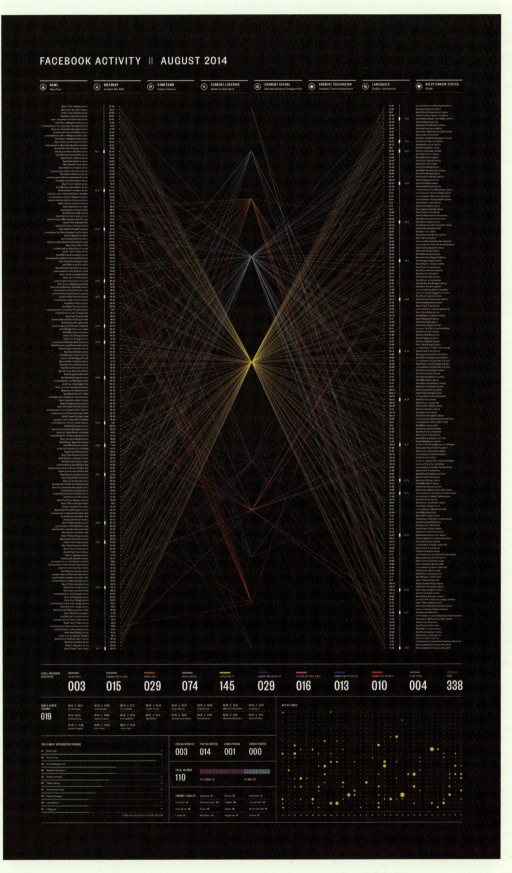

Facebook activity

As a frequent user of Facebook, I wanted to analyze my Facebook activity and the people that I interacted with during the month of August 2014. I gathered information based on my activity log and designated each activity according to its category, such as "commenting on someone's status" or "liking someone's photo." I recorded the exact time and date that each event took place in order to display the items in a vertical timeline. Data analysis included the following: my own post activity (status updates and photos, links, or videos posted), newly added friends, top 10 people I interacted most with, total friends I interacted with, friends' locations, and my most active times on Facebook in August.

Fonts used: Founders Grotesk

Software used: Inkjet Printing, Adobe Illustrator and InDesign, Microsoft Excel

Flipping Pixels

How do you usually interact with a magazine? Probably by flipping through pages, looking at glamorous images and neglecting the text. Flipping Pixels is a publication that attempts to deconstruct *WIRED* magazine and transform its content into a book format. Given the experimental nature of project, I want approach the design aspect of the book with the experience of online reading.

Fonts used: Tungsten, Forza, Metric, Tiempos Text

Software used: Inkjet Printing, Adobe Illustrator and InDesign

Outcast

Outcast conceptualizes the drama within a Shakespeare's play, *The Merchant of Venice*, into a newspaper. While the play itself deals with various themes and issues, I wanted to emphasize the topics of homosexuality and antisemitism within my publication. While the former is addressed explicitly in the play with the relationship between Antonio and Shylock, the latter is addressed implicitly through the friendship between Antonio and Bassanio. Given the experimental nature of the project, I wanted to design a newspaper that only utilizes typography and infographics, without the use of photography. In doing so, I wish to demonstrate the complex character and overlapping layers of Shakespeare's play.

Fonts used: Domaine, National, Newzald

Software used: Inkjet Printing, Adobe Illustrator and InDesign

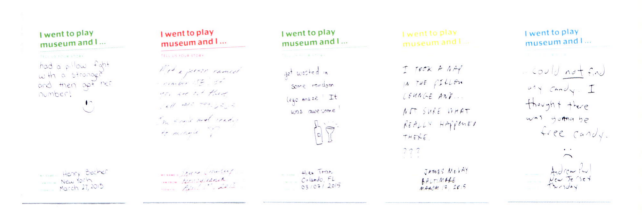

Play Museum

The Play Museum is a place for individuals to escape from the craziness and the bullshit of everyday life. It is a place for visitors to have meaningful and unexpected interactions with others, to engage in various playful game installations, and most importantly, to feel good about being silly. We aim to spark visitors' inner playful adolescence through body play, object play, and imaginative play.

Fonts used: Stag Sans Round, Graphik

Software used: Inkjet Printing, Laser Cutting, Adobe Illustrator and InDesign, Rhino 3D

I've got 99 problems, but _____ ain't one.

Why do you hate going to museums?

It is embarrassing when you _____ at a museum.

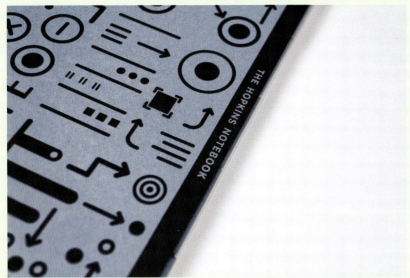

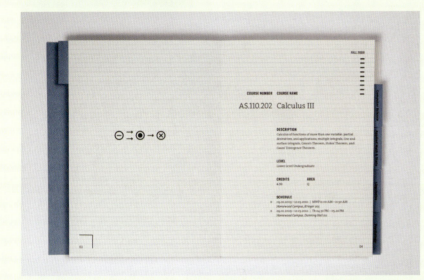

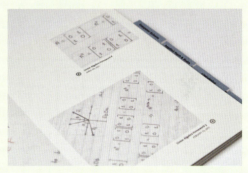

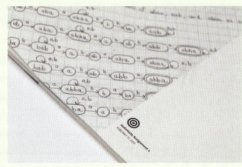

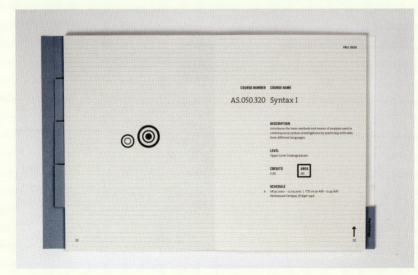

The Hopkins Notebook

This book showcases a collection of scanned documents that I collected over the past 4 years of my undergrad at the Johns Hopkins University. From a huge pile of paper that includes lecture notes, homework, research papers, and exams, I scanned in materials from 9 classes across 5 different fields of study. Then, I studied the visual language of each subject, and, from that, I designed a set of icons for each of the 9 classes.

Fonts used: The Serif, Galaxie Polaris Condensed, National

Production details: Inkjet printing, book binding

Software used: Adobe Illustrator and InDesign

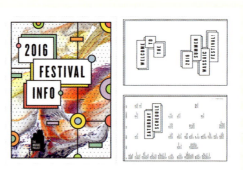

The Wassaic Project

As the 2016 Wassaic Project Design Fellow, I worked closely with the Exhibitions and Program Coordinator and the Design Director to design printed materials— posters, postcards, flyers, and booklets—for the organization's summer programs and festival.

Fonts used: Knockout

Software used: Inkjet Printing, Adobe Illustrator and InDesign

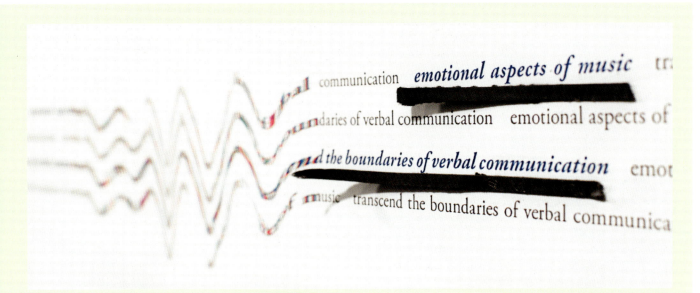

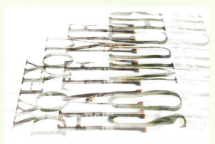

Un-Spoken

This project uses social media as a medium to collect honest anonymous stories from people regarding something he or she would never say face-to-face to someone (whether it be a work colleague, an ex-boyfriend/girlfriend, a parent, a relative, or someone he or she met on the street). This project explores the transformation of words from an online environment to printed media through the use of analog typography in three books featuring the topics of love, friendship, and family. It is the hope that viewers will relate to some of the responses and that they can appreciate the project on an emotional level, in addition to the books as designed objects.

Fonts used: Adobe Garamond

Production details: Inkjet printing, book binding

Software used: Adobe Illustrator, InDesign, and Photoshop

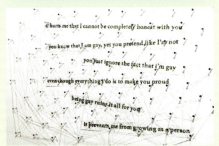

Portfolio Critique by Kris Kiger
Executive Vice President, Executive Creative Director, Design, R/GA
New York, New York

What is your overall impression of this portfolio? What do you like and why?

"I had a sense of an overall high level craft and care taken with his work. He seems very passionate about the details and he's not afraid of diving into the data behind the design. I particularly liked the data visualization piece showing his Facebook usage in Biodiagram. I think it really takes focus to record this kind of data and then put it in a format that gives shape, form, and meaning to it.

This is a skill that will become more important as the world we move through will be capturing, quantifying, and rendering a point of view on things through the lens of datasets. Being able to tell meaningful stories through big data will be a super important skill to have.

I think a strength seen in this body of work is the attention to detail and a range of expression shown through the work. It's smart, thoughtful, and explores a range of styles. It definitely has the right range of work to pique my interest and I want to know more about who he is and what he's interested in doing with the skills he has gained so far in his career."

What advice would you give on this portfolio for areas of improvement?

"Though there is a range in the styles shown, I might like to see even a bit more. Perhaps some experimentation in process, motion, or prototyping. Sometimes through experimenting, happy accidents result in beautiful outcomes. This is definitely an extra credit ask, as there is something to be said for a tight focus and curation of your book to suit a target employer or position. I always like to see the thoughts, sketches, and personal work that's led to the final outcome. I'm interested in the full view of a creative person.

I love the daily UI exploration and challenge he's set up for himself. I'm a big believer you can push your skills into new applications. Giving yourself a daily brief is a wonderful idea. It builds on basic design principles and I love the idea of redesigning things that interest you.

Recognizing this and seeing what he's been able to accomplish, I think a bit deeper exploration on one or two projects could be helpful. Think about a solution from multiple angles or touch points for the audience you're trying to reach. The brand expression and communication manifests itself through the full experience. UI is a huge part of that and it's a viable place to start seeing the full design system that might develop."

Portfolio Spotlight on. . .

Jason Fujikuni

Memo
Digital platform for documenting and sharing memories.
Designed at RISD
Branding, prototype app, film, narrative

First Things First Manifesto poster—Flag/Gun

Propaganda poster about the *First Things First Manifesto* (1964), emphasizing the social responsibility of designers and the national issue of gun control in the United States. Designed to be read both upside-down and right-side-up.

Designed at RISD

Poster, illustration

First Things First Manifesto poster—Glitch

Propaganda poster about the *First Things First Manifesto* (1964), emphasizing the role of inclusion/diversity in the field of design and the increased responsibilities of designers working in the digital/tech age. Upside-down, the phrase 'first things first' can be read in nine different languages. Designed to be read both upside-down and right-side-up.

Designed at RISD

Poster, illustration

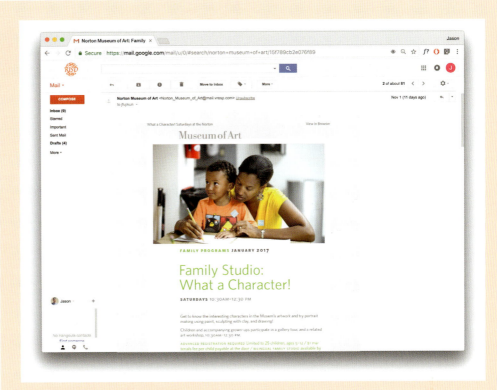

HTML email templates—Norton Museum of Art

New HTML email templates designed for the Norton Museum of Art. The simplified templates employ a modular design that can be customized for a number of email campaigns, and that establish a clear sense of hierarchy and legibility through typography and color.

Designed at The Norton Museum of Art, winter design internship 2017

Digital, typography

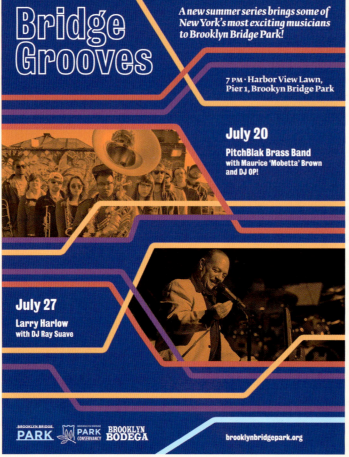

Bridge Grooves—Brooklyn Bridge Park

Signage and event branding design for the summer music series Bridge Grooves held by Brooklyn Bridge Park in 2016.

Designed at Open, summer design internship 2016

Branding, signage, systems

SPAMpaign

Exploration of social media as a curation of content that describes who you are.

Designed at RISD

Identity, illustration, art direction

Message of Hope

Reversible poster diptych spread across Providence the day after the 2016 presidential election.

Designed at RISD

Portfolio Critique by Ida Woldemichael
Associate Creative Director, Wide Eye
Washington D.C.

What is your overall impression of this portfolio? What do you like and why?

"My overall impression is that Jason enjoys creating work that responds to the world around him. SPAMpaign and Message of Hope seemed to do that most successfully.

SPAMpaign is simply successful for putting our mind and curiosity in the space of considering how ones curated social media content relates to who they are. It's a very interesting subject as we think about the way we share information, life updates, and personas with our peers, strangers, or families via this type of media. The use of the SPAM product also makes me think—this is Jason commenting on what he thinks of this: Junk!

With Message of Hope, I love the DIY nature. It's inexpensive, it's creative, it's memorable, and it feels as if it was created quickly, in response to a moment of desperation and sadness."

What advice would you give on this portfolio for areas of improvement?

"Take a closer look at how you resolve for hierarchy via color and typography.

While I enjoyed the First Things First Manifesto Poster-Glitch, and the Brooklyn Grooves project, there a few areas were hierarchy could have been more considered.

For example, in Glitch, I loved the composition. The use of distorted type was great, and reflected back to some of the feeling that was in the First Things First Manifesto. The addition of the various languages hinting at the role of inclusion and diversity was good—but I wanted it to be clearer. Is there something you're communicating in the way we see them upside down? Does the very small scale of them in comparison to the larger type mean something too?

In Brooklyn Grooves, there is interesting color, photo style, and crops. As I got closer the goal seemed two fold: (1) how to educate the visitor on park rules and navigation, and (2) how to promote the event. While the signage to communicate both live on the same plane, it's important to present the information as simply and clearly as possible. How can they feel of the same family, but of different moments? I see an opportunity to make the content around way finding and park rules to feel more evergreen and similar stylistically. I also see an opportunity to make the Bridge Grooves work more playful, and have stronger visual contrast whether via an alternative background color or typeface in contrast to the rules/way finding."

Portfolio Spotlight on. . .

Julia Whitley

Urban Farm Magazine *re-branding*

The concept behind this editorial rebranding is a collision of the words *Urban* and *Farm*. Steering towards millennial consumers who are eco-friendly and strive for minimalist lifestyles, I focused on using a clean design, the incorporation of bright, fresh images, and a wood-cut style of type. Seed paper was incorporated in the magazine pull out as well as the business cards so the owner could plant both of those things and get wildflowers instead of just throwing it away.

Fonts: Sutro and Avenir

Paper: Craft, Seed paper, Recycled Cardstock

Personal branding

My personal branding idea is simple, but with a clear message. To my friends and family, I am known as Jules. Not something usually used in a professional setting, but still gives me an iconic design and striking visual. The contrast of the colors, and their overlay reflects what I desire my overall portfolio to be—dynamic, clean, and striking.

Fonts: Aktiv Grotesk and Sentinel

Created through Moo.com with raised spot gloss ink on the jewel sections

Logo book

Through my time in college, I had designed a collection of 15 different logos for various projects. For presenting to future employers, I decided to design a book of them based on my personal branding and also showing their use not just on their own but with different backgrounds and giving each their own description.

Fonts: Aktiv Grotesk and various

Printed and bound at a local printing company in Stillwater, Oklahoma

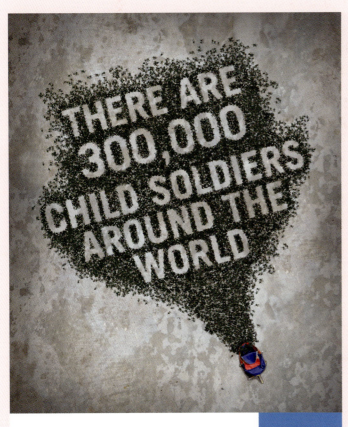

Child Soldiers Awareness poster

There are over 300,000 child soldiers around the world today. This startling fact is portrayed through toy soldiers, something that both represents children and war. I used over a thousand soldiers, photographed them, and placed them to reveal the words. Below the image is text talking about this issue and how one can help.

Created entirely from photographed toy soldiers and Adobe Photoshop

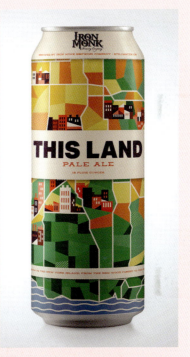

This Land Pale Ale

As part of a local beer can design competition based on the concept of an Oklahoma summer, this design focused on Woody Guthrie, a famous musician and Oklahoma native. His most famous song pays tribute to the American landscape and its vast differences and that is what is portrayed in the design representing the landscape of Oklahoma. This design won and was created into an actual beer label.

Fonts used: Aktiv Grotesk and varius

Printed on a beer label. I also created a poster version printed on textured art paper and hung with a simple wooden magnetic frame.

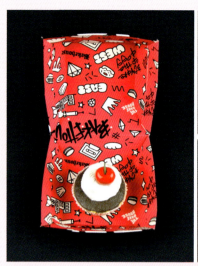

Bakehouse

The Bakehouse is a bakery based on 90s hip hop and rap. Its two locations, Los Angelos and Brooklyn, are hubs for the 90s hip hop movements. Its design focused on incorporating that style, both looking historically at the 90s and also thinking about the culture behind hip hop. I designed all the collateral and copy for this project.

Fonts: self-created and Din

Clamshell mockup from The Dieline

Lasercutter used for the coffee sleeve

Tracing paper used for the wax paper design

Props from Hobby Lobby

Stickers created from stickermule.com

Portfolio Critique by Lara McCormick
Creative Director, Exploratorium
San Francisco, California

What is your overall impression of this portfolio? What do you like and why?

"It's amazing! I love the variety of project types, both in content and execution. Julia has a strong grasp of the essential design foundations: color, composition, and typography. And I love the focus on social responsibility. This reveals a bit about the type of person Julia is.

The Pale Ale project stands out the most. It's clean, colorful, and bold. The illustration is playful and feels just right. It also covers two different touch points, packaging and web design. This shows me the student is able to take a look and feel and apply it across different mediums consistently.

I also love Julia's business card, particularly the back! I would want this in my hand if I met with her for an interview.

Julia's typography solutions demonstrate a nice variety across all her projects and each looks different from the next. I've seen portfolios where a typeface is used across different projects and everything starts to look the same. This definitely isn't the case with Julia's work."

What advice would you give on this portfolio for areas of improvement?

"I recommend placing designs in situ, so you get a sense of context at-a-glance. Especially web projects. If they're in a browser or monitor I know exactly what I'm looking at. Having said that, don't go overboard. Julia's Bakehouse project has a shot that could be improved (shown above) by taking the pattern from the interior of the box and zooming in, so that I can really dig into all the awesome moments going on in the design."

Portfolio Spotlight on. . .

June Shin

*Scripting Allographs** (MFA Graphic Design Graduate Thesis, 2017)

Scripting Allographs* examines typographic principles and their pervasive impact on ways of seeing and making through design. This body of work demonstrates the many faces of typography and type design and the way they inform allographic thinking. It employs type as the primary tool and medium for scripting possibilities, embracing their differences, idiosyncrasies, and imperfections. Beginning with a focus on close observation of small details and ending with an approach that invites and celebrates variability, this thesis offers a glimpse into a design practice from the lens of a typographer, type designer, and educator.

Scripting—the term "script" has more than one meaning: handwriting, calligraphy, a writing system, a predefined sequence of events such as a musical score or a screenplay, or a programming language as in computing. Its verb form, to script, then, can mean to write a text, draw a letterform, or devise a plan that determines a course of action.

Allographs—an allograph, a linguistics term, is every possible manifestation of a letter: A, a, *A, a*, A, *a*, and all hand-written or hand-lettered forms. By foregrounding subtle differences found among variants of a single idea, this term points to the notion of infinite possibility. How many different ways can you write or draw something? The potential is exhilarating.

Fonts used: Neue Haas Unica (Monotype), Canela (Commercial Type), Tiempos (Klim), Miller (Carter & Cone), Input Sans (DJR)

Software used: Adobe Creative Suite

Printed at Allegra (Providence, Rhode Island)

Hand-sewn at Hope Bindery (Pawtucket, Rhode Island)

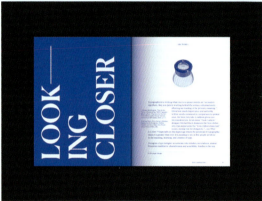

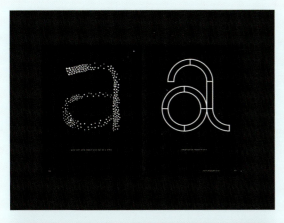

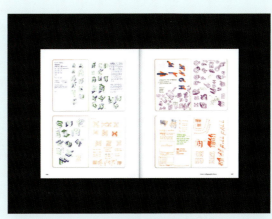

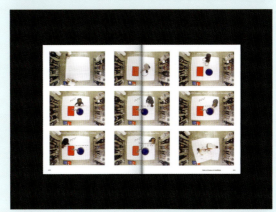

Identity for Alhambra, Generalife, and Albayzín, Granada

Alhambra, Generalife, and Albayzín, Granada, is a UNESCO World Heritage site in Spain. This speculative identity project, inspired by the mesmerizing ornamentation and geometric patterns found on the walls and ceilings of the Alhambra Palace, includes: logomark and logotype with custom type, a full-page magazine ad, a website design, letterhead and envelope, a book about the site as well as the World Heritage Convention, and a brand identity guide.

Fonts used: Fedra Sans and Fedra Serif (Typotheque)

Software used: Adobe Creative Suite

Software used: Robofont

Hand-sewn book

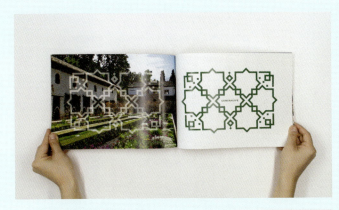

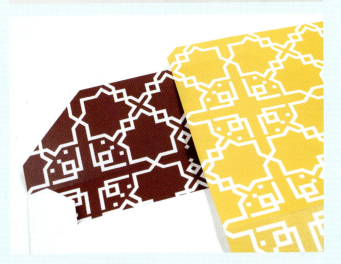

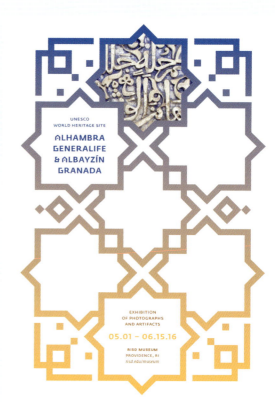

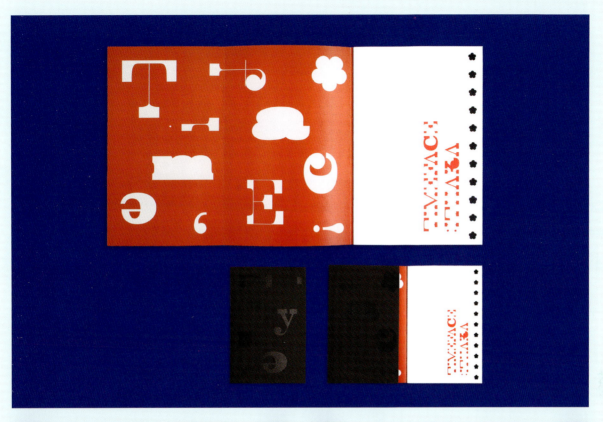

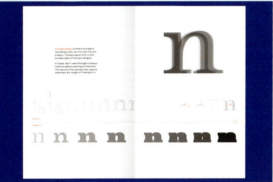

Timeface

Timeface is an infographic typeface that visualizes the time investment and logic involved in type design. With the memory of my design process for my latest typeface Ithaka (2016) still fresh in my mind and the numerous UFO (Unified Font Object) files still on my hard drive, I created a sequel typeface in which the amount of time I spent on designing a character for Ithaka determined the weight of its Timeface counterpart. Those letters that required the most effort—the "control characters," for instance—gained so much weight that they lost their white spaces and counters, ending up as blobs. The specimen-like booklet explains the logic behind the typeface, providing a glimpse into the inner workings of type design. This conceptual typeface is at once a record of my thinking and my process of designing Ithaka and an invitation to the secret club that is the tiny world of type design.

Fonts do not just drop from the sky, yet not many people realize there is a designer or a team of designers behind each one. Even for graphic designers, type design is a particularly specialized niche field whose inner workings are mysterious and whose craft is often overlooked. Type design takes time. It is a laborious process that demands patience, persistence, and a hell of a lot of love for type. As a type designer myself, I wanted to make a typeface about type design in order to share my process as well as my love for letterforms and the type design practice. While Timeface is based on my process for one particular typeface, Ithaka, it also provides insights into some of the mechanics of type design. It is my hope that this experimental typeface, with its exuberantly eccentric forms, offers a fresh take on reimagining what a typeface can be or do, as well as pure joy.

Fonts used: Ithaka (June Shin)

Software used: Robofont

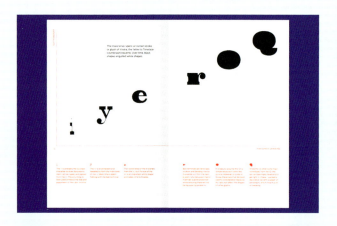

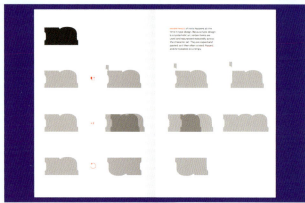

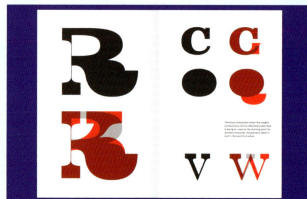

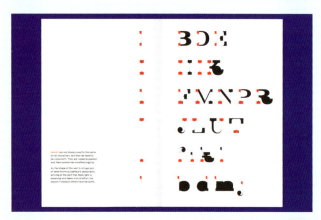

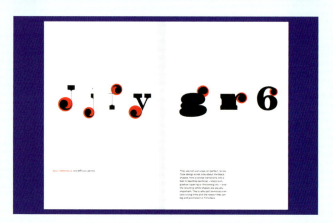

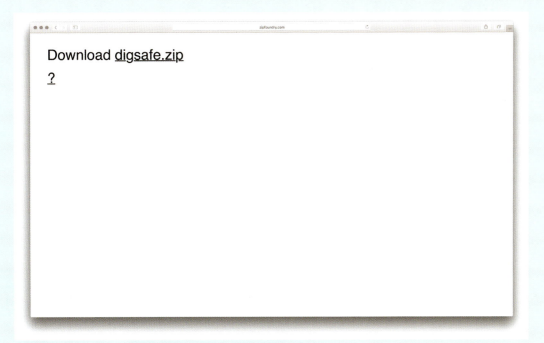

Zip Foundry is an online publishing platform founded by June Shin (RISD GD MFA '17), a member of the Experimental Publishing Studio, led by Paul Soulellis, at the Rhode Island School of Design.

Here, stories are published in the form of zip files. Once downloaded and decompressed, each of the zip file's many components will reveal a different aspect of the story waiting to be heard, seen, and read.

These zip files are packaged raw meat. You may cook and consume it however you wish. You get out of it what you want.

<

Download digsafe.zip

?

Digsafe.zip

Utility workers' marks are colorful spray-painted letters and symbols commonly found on the streets in urban environments. DigSafe.zip brings these familiar yet overlooked marks to the foreground. The title comes from Dig Safe System, Inc., a clearinghouse that notifies utility companies of planned excavations.

DigSafe.zip comprises ten files in various formats: a GIF, a text file, a font file, a Google Maps link, a few PDFs, a folder of JPEGs, and two audio recordings. Ranging from a group of photographs of the marks and a font made from digitizing them, to a recording of ambient sound collected around construction sites, each item provides additional context to the stories behind this banal subject. By offering ten perspectives rather than a single narrative, DigSafe.zip invites the reader to uncover them in any sequence or combination. Visit Zip Foundry at zipfoundry.com to download DigSafe.zip.

Fonts used: Digsafe (June Shin), Atlas Grotesk (Commercial Type)

Software used: Adobe InDesign, Robofont

Do you ever use black?

Yeah, when we make a mistake.
Because you won't see black.
Black is just a whiteout.

when we make a mistake

Do people lose lives?

Absolutely. Oh, absolutely.
It happens. It happens.

If you make a mistake and you hit it,
you're not gonna survive.
It only takes one tenth of one amp to kill you.

It happens.

Do you feel tremendous pressure?

No, no.

No? Because you're highly skilled?

No, it's like crossing a street.
At some point, you pay attention to what you do.
I know where all the stuff is,
just by looking at that kind of stuff,
you know what I mean?

...it's like crossing a street.

Everything else freezes,
so you need to be at least 5 ft. down.
The water mains have to be at least 5 ft. down,
the sewer lines, typically at 5 ft.
And then they'll go 10 ft...20 ft...-

You mean literally freeze because it's cold.

Yeah, the water mains will freeze.
Communication doesn't freeze.

What?

Communication does not freeze.

Communication does not freeze.

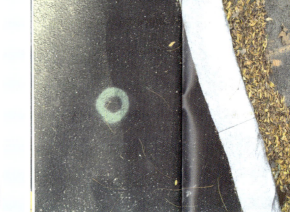

HOW ACCURATE ARE THEY? IT'S JUST A GUIDELINE TO FOLLOW.

THE ORANGE WILL COST YOU EVERY THING YOU EVER OWNED.

THE YELLOW WOULD LITERALLY BLOW A PERFECT TRENCH.

THE BLUE, IT JUST MAKES A MESS.

THE RED MARKS WILL KILL YOU. OH, YEAH. NO KIDDING.

Portfolio Critique by Gail Anderson
Gail Anderson, Chair, BFA Design and BFA Advertising,
Creative Director, Visual Arts Press
School of Visual Arts
New York, New York

What is your overall impression of this portfolio? What do you like and why?

"I am blown away by June's portfolio, period. If this is indeed student work, and she's only a year out of grad school, then I'm excited to see what she'll produce five years from now. Actually, I'm excited to see what she's up to right now.

June's portfolio is a model book. I get a strong sense of who she is and where her interests lie. The obligatory Alhambra website seems like a bit of a throwaway, but otherwise, the components of each project are carefully crafted and nicely presented.

June has a great eye for typographic pairings and excellent editorial design skills. She is clearly able to construct strong pages. I would love to have a hard copy of her thesis book. So impressive."

What advice would you give on this portfolio for areas of improvement?

"Can June give ME some advice?

Otherwise, all I can say is keep following your muse, June. You seem to have your head screwed on straight and know what you want.

Make sure to take a break and look up. Shoot pictures, keep a journal or a sketchbook. Get your hands dirty."

Portfolio Spotlight on. . .

Linnea Taylor

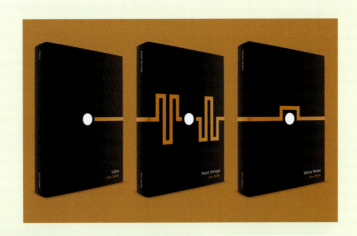

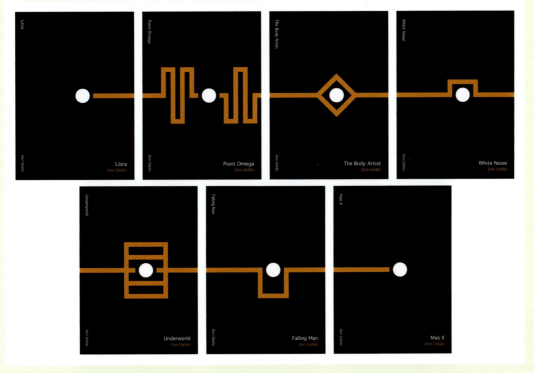

"Don Delillo: Time"—covers

As an American novelist, playwright, and essayist, Don Delillo has covered a wide variety of subjects—including nuclear war, the impending digital age, and the JFK assassination just to name a few. As a well-regarded cult writer, he has described his writing to be focused on "living in dangerous times." With an impressive and diverse list of over 15 novels, Delillo's work carries an unsettling and honest portrayal of the pressures of the clock. This book series is a literal representation of the often obscure interaction humans have with time, its meaning, and its relation to others—whether it be a desire to slow it down, to expand it, or to avoid it completely.

This project was a 3-book series exploration, based on an author of our choice, directed by John Gall at the School of Visual Arts. I am a big Don Delillo fan so I expanded it to more of his books with a cohesive theme he uses thought many novels: time and the paths it can take. Each book cover and spine was created in Adobe Illustrator and mocked-up in Photoshop.

Fonts used: Geneva—Regular

Rendered by a PSD created by www.psdcovers.com

"FINE"—Section Opener

In a city filled with countless galleries, museums, pop-up shows, open studies, and more, it can be hard to keep up with the ever-expanding art scene of New York CIty. *Fine* provides extensive insight into the Big Apple's creative landscape for both artistic experts and newcomers alike. Stay up-to-date on the most anticipated shows of the season, as well as the fleeting ones that you just cannot miss. Meet the upcoming visionaries new to the field and learn about the classics that you might have missed. Whether it's the white walls of Chelsea or the warehouses of Brooklyn—*Fine* is here to make sure you never stop discovering the very best New York City has to offer.

Fine is the result of a project to conceive a full fictitious magazine created under the direction of Robert Best at the School of Visual Arts. Based on the New York City art scene, it contains real articles, shows, artists, and artwork based and appearing in the city. This entire magazine was created in Adobe InDesign, the cover was created in Adobe Illustrator, and mocked up in Adobe Photoshop.

Fonts used: Work Sans—Regular, SemiBold, Bold; Univers LT Std Oblique, Bold Oblique, Roman, Bold, Extra Black, Roman; Syncopate Regular

Photoshop Magazine mock-up package found on Behance

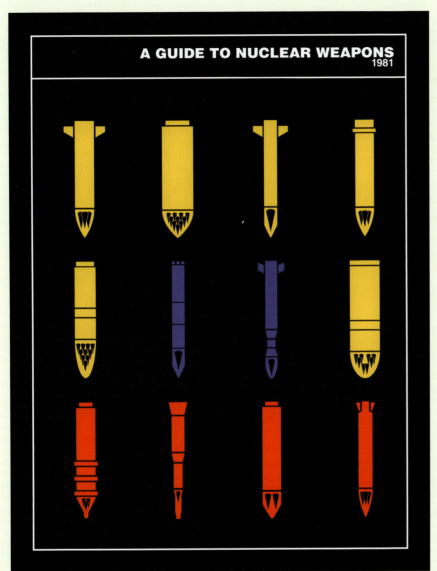

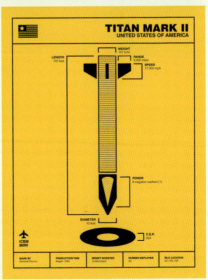

"A Guide to Nuclear Weapons—1981"—Titan Mark II

In 1980, concerns about nuclear war and interest in nuclear disarmament grew due to heightened cold war tensions following the Iranian Revolution, the Soviet invasion of Afghanistan, and the expanding study of strategic nuclear weapons throughout the world. This formed a demand for information about the nuclear arms race and Dr. Paul Rogers of The School of Peace Studies at the University of Bradford responded. From his guide to the major nuclear weapon systems then available to the world's nuclear powers grew an infographic poster series—consisting of accurate structural representation and classification, production and fiscal information, as well as speed, range, and power capabilities.

At SVA, Dan Blackman directed us to create a project consisting of physical aspects based on a book, pamphlet, or any piece of writing really. After finding the guide to nuclear weapons, I created a series of posters in Adobe Illustrator based on the information it contained, and also on what it did not. The set is then to be held within a model rocket tube, which I found and painted black to match the full-series poster. The production photos are real-life images shot by photographer Kyle Rudd with the posters overlayed in Adobe Photoshop.

Fonts used: Helvetica LT Std Black, Bold

97

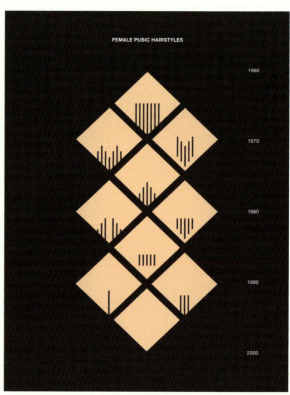

"The Bush is Back"—infographic page

Before the rise of the bikini in the 1960's and 1970's, women only shaved their pubic hair because of personal preference. However, the pressure to be smooth overpowered and, until recent years, was seen as the norm, often being criticized by media and social constructs if otherwise. However, through the recent feminist revival not only have many women began going "natural" again, many celebrities and adult actresses have spoken out about it with much support. For women, it encompasses the idea that women are in control of their bodies and empowers women through making decisions on how to maintain the female body as a personal choice, not a societal one. With inspiration from the 60's and 70's such as color palette, type, and imagery, the concept of "The Bush is Back" was born.

At the direction of Dan Blackman at SVA, we were to choose a *New York Magazine* special issue theme and create our own cover. In choosing "Special Double Issue: Sex," I decided not to focus on the physical act but another aspect around sex—pubic hair. In turn, I created a cover, along with an additional infographic of female pubic hair styles through the decades, in Adobe Illustrator and mocked-up the final versions in Adobe Photoshop.

Fonts used: Helvetica Neue Bold; Unique Regular

Website portfolio

Entire responsive site is designed, hand-coded in HTML/CSS/JavaScript, and populated/maintained by Linnea Taylor.

"I want my SVA!"—invitation teaser

Whether you're *pretty in pink* or rock a *raspberry beret*—rewind a few decades for this party at SVA! Hosted by the totally tubular Board of Directors, along with the raddest art school around, the School of Visual Arts, invites you to bust out your neon gear for this 80s style Annual Party. Rock a single glove made of glitter, tease your hair, any way you want to rock—all staff, faculty, and friends are welcome. We're going way back, but now's our time to show you why everyone is saying, "I want my SVA!"

Art Director: Ryan Durinick

Copyrighted by: School of Visual Arts

Fonts used: SF Digital Readout Medium Oblique; VCR OSD Mono; Coffee Service Regular; Hurme Geometric Sans No.2 Regular, Bold

Raw green screen footage keyed out in AfterEffects using Keylight and additional motion masking

Composed with audio and backgrounds in Premiere

Created flashing time stamp in AfterEffects and overlaid

Multiple adjustment layers added in Premiere (Wave Warp, Noise, and footage overlay)

"All-Star Serial Killers"—full set

Fonts used: Avenir Next—Bold; AG Old Face—Bold/Medium/Regular; Trade Gothic LT Std—Bold No.2; Franklin—Heavy; Frutiger—Black; Helvetica—Bold/Bold Condensed; Reznik—Black Italic; Micro FLF—Bold; Arial—Bold/Black; Helvetica Neue—Heavy/Condensed Bold; Trade Gothic LH—Bold Extended; Zurich—Bold Extended/Bold; Napoli—Extra Bold; ITC Franklin Gothic—Demi Condensed Italic

Created in Adobe Photoshop with drop shadow effect on all cards

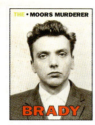 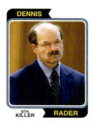   
    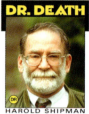

Fonts used: Arial—Black; Franklin—Demi; ITC Franklin Gothic—Demi Condensed Italic

Production Techniques: Found an image of a foil package and single razor—masked both out individually; Placed package design (created in illustrator) over the foil package; Set the package design to 'multiply' and made a clipping mask.

Foil package, razor, and cards all have drop shadows

Found an image of a clear card case and masked it out in Photoshop; Placed a single layer of the masked card case at 20% opacity with drop shadow; Placed a card file on top of card case layer with drop shadow; Duplicated the card case layer, removed the drop shadow, set to 'linear burn' and brought it to front (over the card).

Berkowitz

Fonts used: Frutiger—Black;
Arial—Bold / Black /
Regular; Akzidenz-Grotesk
BQ—Bold Condensed

Haigh

Fonts used: Avenir Next—
Bold; Garage Gothic—Black;
Futura Std—Bold Oblique /
Bold; Century Old Style—Bold

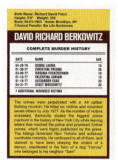

Zodiac

Fonts used: AG Old Face—Bold / Medium / Regular;
Helvetica Neue LT Std—Condensed

Serial killer cases, open or closed, continue to fascinate law enforcement agents, psychologists, and fanatics of all things morbid long after the crimes occur. While all vicious acts of these murderers end the same, there are many variables in their personalities, motives, and execution of crimes that distinguish them in time. To organize such a wide-ranging and diverse collection of information, these All-Star Serial Trading Cards highlight profiles, types of murders and their victims, and motives behind such horrendous acts. All are designed to display "stats" of each killer corresponding to the decade in which they committed these crimes and provide a quick reference for ominous data.

Portfolio Critique by Rietje Becker
Creative Director, Soulsight
Chicago, Illinois

What is your overall impression of this portfolio? What do you like and why?

"Linnea's book is varied in its subject matter and thoughtful in its execution. I like that she is not afraid to take on controversial topics. One of my favorites is her *Fine* magazine project, which includes some of her best layout options and successfully uses found media. I would have liked to see her push this project even further. Would you change it in an interactive version? And how? Are there additional print ways this could have been expressed? I think Linnea's strength is in distilling subject matter into thoughtful iconography. She does this in both her Don DeLillo and *New York Magazine* projects."

What advice would you give on this portfolio for areas of improvement?

"This book would benefit from more variation in design styles. Currently, a few of the projects use a collaged look (Trading cards, SVA Annual Party, Fine Magazine) while the rest use a similar style of vector iconography and line elements (*New York Magazine*, portfolio, Nuclear, Don DeLillo). This is especially visible across the more editorial projects. Would be great to see what other design aesthetics Linnea is able to express. Typographically, she uses mostly staid classics and would benefit from exploring some newer type foundries. I recognize this is tough on a student's budget, but will make her work look more current and her type more expressive. Additionally, it would have been nice to see more interactive/web work, given her experience in that area."

Portfolio Spotlight on. . .

Masha Vainblat

Anatolia Winery branding

Anatolia is an artisanal Greek winery. The strong agricultural roots in the region of Anatolia allow for an exquisite wine tasting experience. The branding concept derives from a thyrsus—a vine or ivy leaf covered wand with a pinecone top carried by Dionysus, the Greek god of wine and chaos. There are seven Greek varietals which were specifically chosen for the rich artisanal flavors.

Fonts used: Intellecta Roman Tall, Bulmer MT

Software used: Adobe InDesign, Photoshop, and Illustrator, LiveSurface Context (for mock-ups)

Linum Kinito branding and package design

Linum presents the Kinito hotspot phone case. With the flip of a switch, WiFi can be accessed in non-reception areas. The concept of this project was to repurpose and brand a hardware item: *linum*, which translates to network; *kinito,* which is the Greek translation for mobile and is reminiscent of kinetic energy and motion.

Fonts used: Baskerville Bold, Univers 45 Light

Production details: The silk textured and silkscreened packaging is handmade using paper-on-board technique. Silk screen printed at the SVA print shop.

Photographed by Ramon Martinez

Software used: Adobe Illustrator

Sonny Rollins LP series

Sonny Rollins is a famous jazz musician from Harlem. Whenever he felt he was reaching a peak in his career, Sonny would go on sabbatical to travel and rehearse his craft. The concept behind the design defines the mystery and spontaneity in improvisational music that is jazz. The imagery and graphics used for this design are visual fragments of some of Rollins' most famous recordings from each album.

Fonts used: Univers U47, Univers 67 Bold Condensed, Univers 45 Light

Production details: Printed in SVA Computer Lab

Photographed by Ramon Martinez.

Software used: Adobe Illustrator and Photoshop

SVA Continuing Education website redesign

Visual Arts Press Internship work. SVA's Continuing Education department requested a website redesign for their course registration page. In collaboration with Eric Corriel, Michael J Walsh, and Declan Van Welie, a visual thumbnail approach and custom icon system was designed and developed which led to heightened site traffic and increased enrollment for CE courses. http://www.sva.edu/continuing-education.

Fonts used: Museo Sans

Production details: Developed by VAP by Eric Corriel and Declan Van Welie

Software used: Adobe Illustrator and InDesign

Current Course Finder Page

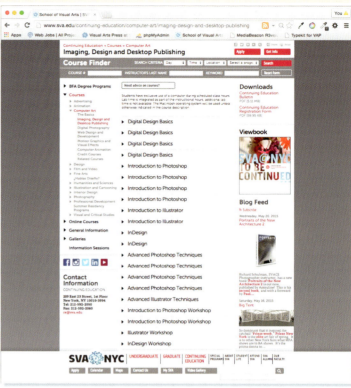

Course Finder Redesign
App Thumbnails

Desktop View
Landing Page

Mobile View
Landing Page

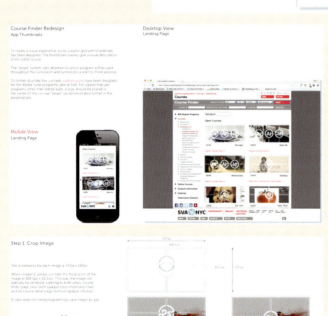

Course Finder Redesign
Hover State Option 1

Desktop View

Mobile View

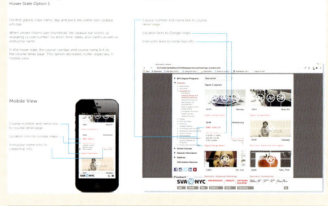

Step 1: Crop Image

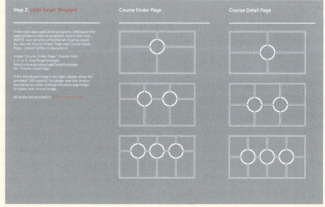

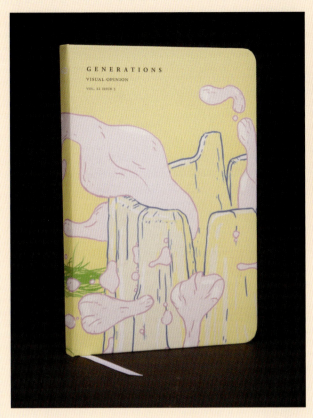

Visual Opinion *Magazine*

SVA Student-run publication. The *Visual Opinion* is SVA's student-run magazine which showcases the best talent from the college's undergraduate and graduate majors and departments. The *VO*'s mission is to give students the opportunity to share their talent as well as inspire their peers to create wonderful art. This tri-semester publication gathers and curates artwork based on given themes for each issue. The *VO* has been distributing campus wide for over 20 years. With new student staff members each year, the magazine strives to leave a legacy for many more years to come.

Fonts used: Futura

Production details: Printed by Thomas Group Printing

Photographed by Ramon Martinez

Software used: Adobe InDesign

Portfolio Critique by Ryan Scott Tandy
Product Design Manager, Instagram
San Francisco, California

What is your overall impression of this portfolio? What do you like and why?

"I'm impressed by the range of projects in Masha's portfolio that span branding to print to digital. Masha's attention to detail, use of imagery and sharp typography in her print/branding projects specifically stand out as her strengths.

The Kinito project is my favorite piece from the portfolio not only because of the well executed packaging or custom type, but because it connects back to a core problem people have with connectivity."

What advice would you give on this portfolio for areas of improvement?

"Anatolia Winery—branding

Great use of typography and color throughout this project, but perhaps these elements could work even harder.

Consider introducing stronger hierarchy in the different type sizes to create a bolder contrast.
Linum Kinito—branding and package design

Love the custom typography work, it would be awesome to use some of these line elements from each stroke to create other visual patterns/artifacts for use elsewhere in the project.

Imagine creating a texture from the WiFi lines that could be layered on the inside of the box.
Sonny Rollins LP series—package design

Great use of color and visual texture on these, they work well at drawing you in and creating a sense of wonder.

Reusing the same visuals for the label of the record feels redundant. Try exploring other iterations that use the circular shape of the label or something that really uses the bold colors of each sleeve.
SVA Continuing Education—website redesign

This is a huge improvement from the all-text list of classes in the original website. The new focus on visual thumbnails gives you a lot more context and sense of what the class is about.

There is still a lot of work to do here in making these thumbnails more usable. Currently the grid of thumbnails isn't very scannable. The lockup of each thumbnail could be more clear as would giving prominence to a key action.

I appreciate the idea behind the icon system for each thumbnail as they do provide context and value to the student browsing. That said, heavy line art and icons stand out far more than the imagery content and name of the class which are the primary function of the page. Consider trying alternate lockups where these icons can sit nested within the image."

Portfolio Spotlight on. . .

Yejee Pae

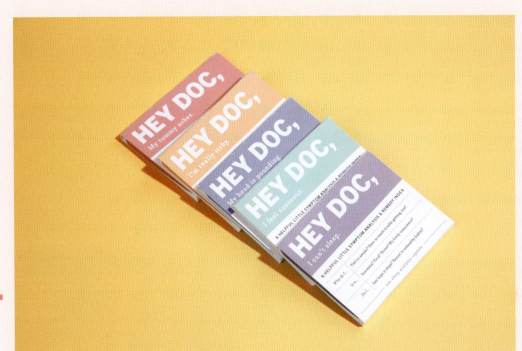

Hey Doc—package design

Hey Doc, is a conceptual packaged solution to our everyday bodily issues. Whether it's a headache, stomach ache, itch, nausea, or a sleepless night, Hey Doc, is a small capsule that you swallow which contains a microbot. As it travels through your system, it will analyze what's going on in your body and send you a notification straight to your phone in a matter of hours and let you know what the problem is, and what you can do to remedy it without unnecessary prescription drugs and painkillers. Made for a Communication Design class at the School of Visual Arts under the instruction of Ryan Dunn and Wyeth Hansen. Printed at home on heavyweight paper with an inkjet printer. Conceptual pills made from Play-Doh.

Fonts used: DIN Text Black, Bodoni Egyptian

Software used: Adobe Illustrator

Invisible Cities—book design

Varying sized books hand-bound into a single book to encompass the mathematical structure and creative vision of Italo Calvino's *Invisible Cities*. We were assigned to rethink the way a book is read, and so I set on creating five separate books that are meticulously bound to turn into one single book; because, in actuality, all the cities that Marco Polo describes to Kublai Khan is are actually the city of Venice, his home. The first book, introducing the author, and the last book, being the last conversation had between Marco Polo and Kublai Khan, the books in between are 3 groups of cities that Italo Calvino describes: Cities & Memory, Cities & Desire, and Thin Cities. Made for a Communication Design class at the School of Visual Arts under the instruction of Ryan Dunn and Wyeth Hansen. Printed and bound at home, linen paper on an inkjet printer. Bound with doubled white sewing thread.

Fonts used: GT Sectra and Avante Garde

Software used: Adobe Illustrator and InDesign

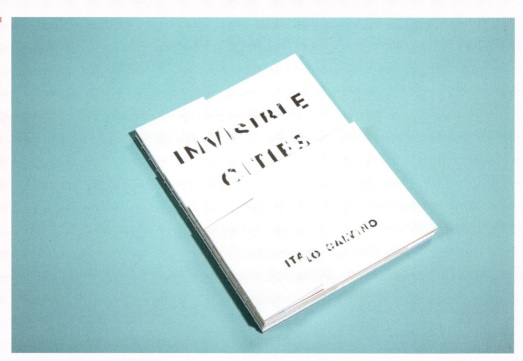

Shits & Stairs—board game design

Shits & Stairs is a remake on the childhood classic of Chutes & Ladders, with a twist. Intended for young adults, this game is designed to get you hammered out of your mind, and compete with your friends to climb to the top and win at life. Each "stair" is a life achievement and each "shit slide" is. . . well. . . shitty. There are chance tiles that will either make you drink, hate life, or turn friends into enemies. Four shot glass playing pieces are included with the board—alcohol not included. Soon to be a classic in every millennial's home. Made for a Senior Design Portfolio class at the School of Visual Arts under the instruction of Ken Deegan and BK Harvey. Nine 12"x12" white acrylic boards manufactured at Canal Plastics. Shot glasses sourced from Flying Tiger Copenhagen and hand painted with glass paint. Board game tiles, cards, and card box printed at home on an inkjet printer with Moab double-sided matte paper.

Fonts used: Graphik Font Family

Software used: Adobe Illustrator

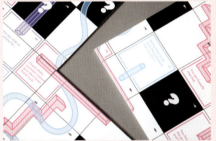

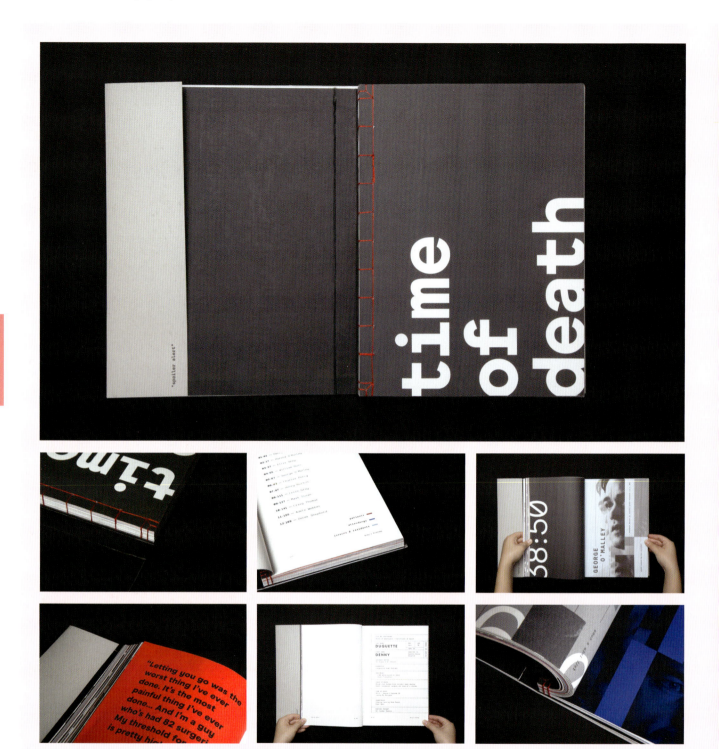

Time of Death—book design

Time of Death is a hand-bound art book that compiles twelve of the most heartbreaking character deaths in chronological order from the show Grey's Anatomy. Each section consists of a short bio, images, a custom death certificate, and quotes that encompass the life and death of each character. Made for a Senior Design Portfolio class at the School of Visual Arts under the instruction of Ken Deegan and BK Harvey. The assignment was intended to convert a lowbrow or guilty pleasure TV show and transform it into a highbrow art book. Printed at home on crest paper, colored papers, and vellum with an inkjet printer. Bound together using a Japanese stab binding method with a custom handmade folding hardcover with doubled red sewing thread.

Fonts used: Modern Era Font Family (Mono & Sans Serif)

Software used: Adobe InDesign

Portfolio Critique by Emily Wengert
Group Vice President, User Experience, Huge Inc.
Brooklyn, New York

What is your overall impression of this portfolio? What do you like and why?

"I love the sense of humor in everything shared—particularly the Shits & Stairs board game and Hey Doc packaging. This shows me someone who pays attention to details and how their work is experienced and isn't just designing for beauty or art. A great designer understands that content/storytelling matters. There's even sense of humor in the Grey's Anatomy high brow book, and I love how high touch it feels. What a fun assignment to take a low brow guilty pleasure and make it high design!

I often jump straight to looking at someone's work. I want to know if their design can speak for itself. In this case, I just started looking at the images, and it was great to be able to understand what the product or idea was without having to be told."

What advice would you give on this portfolio for areas of improvement?

"I think there's a lot of empathy built into these designs, particularly the Hey Doc packaging. Clearly, there was effort put toward understanding what people might be feeling as they swallow a camera pill and try to reassure them, while also adding levity at a stressful time. I'd highlight your process more as you package these assets. Knowing your thinking, things that didn't work, how you tested your ideas, and why you landed where you did helps a hiring manager know how you think. It's never about loving an individual piece—hiring someone is always about whether the manager can picture having your way of thinking applied to the problems they are trying to tackle.

The hardest thing when looking at a graduate's portfolio is understanding who else helped. Team projects can mean I'll see fantastic creativity coming from a group of 4, but I won't know if the candidate I'm reviewing contributed the parts that are winning me over (or if they were the ones napping on the couch while everyone else got shit done). I think these were all individual pieces, which is super impressive to be strong at the writing and the design, so I'd call out your role more.

The other suggestion I'd make is to know who you're sending your portfolio to and focus on (or link to) the pieces you think matter most to them. As someone who works at the intersection between physical and digital and is looking for technology innovation, I would like the work but not bring in to interview—not because it isn't strong work (because it is) but because I can't glimpse the kind of thinking I most need to see. That's often the biggest gap between a graduating student's portfolio and someone with 1 or 2 years of work behind them. A student has oftentimes used the school environment to explore lots of things and learn what they love and what they don't. Make your portfolio a showcase for what you love to do—not just what you have done. That way you catch the right person's eye with your thinking."

113

4

Getting hired

How do you stand out from the crowd and get your foot in the door for that important on-site interview? How do you create an effective resume and cover letter to accompany your portfolio in order to catch the attention of a recruiter or hiring manager and get an interview? Then, once you're in the door, what kind of questions should you expect? How do you prepare for the interview?

This chapter will help you prepare with three clinics: *Resume*, *Cover letter*, and *Interview clinic*. These sections include advice on writing an effective resume and cover letter geared towards the design industry as well as sample prompts for answers to frequently asked questions during the hiring process.

Resume clinic

Creating the perfect design resume should be a semester-long design course. A successful resume takes a balance of writing, editing, formatting, as well as design, typographic hierarchy, layout, composition, color, and branding.

Writing your resume

Include the basics:

From a writing perspective, your resume needs to be tailored to the design position and the company. In the header of your resume, include the basics: your name, contact information (email and phone number; address is optional), and your portfolio URL.

Emphasize key words:

Include your relevant experience from on-campus jobs, internships, and design-related activities. Begin with the most relevant experience in chronological order, for example, start by describing your role in your summer internships, followed by jobs outside of the industry. Use action verbs to describe your contributions to the company during your internships, rather than using the pronoun "I."

If you're lacking formal internship experience, consider highlighting relevant experience as independent work. For example, if you had freelance projects where you branded your neighborhood's yoga studio, designed your university's newspaper, or designed the logo for your friend's band and designed posters for their shows, consider including that experience on your resume.

If you're not sure where to start, try working with your university's Writing Center or Career Center to get advice on how to write about your professional experience.

Spell check!

Always spell check your resume and have a trusted friend or family member check your resume. There is no faster way to kill your chance of getting invited to an interview than to submit a resume with spelling or grammar mistakes.

Tailor your resume:

If you're applying for multiple jobs, you should have multiple copies of your resume targeting the specific requirements and skills that you can pull from the job description. Highlight what the employer is looking for in your resume.

Use a professional naming convention when you're emailing your resumes to avoid mix-ups. For example, if you're applying to Huge and to R/GA, you might have two different resumes tailored to each job description: MarySmith_HugeInc_Resume2018.pdf and MarySmith_RGA_Resume2018.pdf.

The potential employer should be able to easily skim your list of qualifications. Use action verbs and short bullets to describe each experience accurately and clearly. List accomplishments rather than just describing duties. You may consider including honors and awards relevant to the design industry. For example: having your work published in the 2019 Graphis New Talent Annual is a relevant honor to be included on your resume, save your award for Best Smile in your senior year class for another day.

About references:

Don't list references or write "references available on request" on your resume. It's assumed that you can provide this information when it's time for a reference check. However, be courteous to your references and reach out ahead of time to ask for permission to use them as a reference, along with a copy of your resume and the link to the job description. You may also want to provide your references with a short bullet of accomplishments you want them to mention during the reference check.

Resume writing tips

Sample Action Verbs

Brainstormed

Designed

Developed

Illustrated

Produced

Animated

Prototyped

Researched

Participated

Created

Chaired

Directed

Founded

Initiated

Led

Moderated

Contributed

Collaborated

Prepared

Partnered

Sample Bullets

- Developed identity concepts for a branding and a rebranding project
- Led the development of customized giveaway collateral for a launch event
- Supported the Senior Designer in creating, designing, and producing training materials for an international branding workshop
- Collaborated with creative director, copywriters, and designers to develop a marketing campaign for a large automobile brand
- Designed web and mobile e-commerce prototypes for internal and client-facing reviews
- Developed UI mock-ups, flow diagrams, conceptual diagrams, wireframes, visual mockups, and interactive prototypes for a major fashion brand
- Participated in usability testing, developing user experience standards and requirements
- Conducted competitive analysis in fashion markets to identify emerging trends
- Assisted creative teams with photo shoots and production duties
- Participate in UX and design critiques at all stages of projects
- Attended weekly work-share meetings to present progress on the projects, share inspiration, and gain a deeper understanding of the creative process

Designing your resume

Your resume should reflect your personal brand and your design aesthetic in the choice of typography as well as an understanding of scale and layout in the way that you design the information. Your resume is one of the first pieces of design work that your future employer will see and evaluate. Make sure you choose the right typeface combinations. Consider how your information and typographic hierarchy is established in your layout, and aim for clarity in the hierarchy.

Keep it simple. Use InDesign to set up a grid that allows you to lay out the information with clear typographic hierarchy and consistent alignment. Use a legible typeface with a superfamily of weights so you can streamline the combination of typefaces without overwhelming your resume with too many. Stay away from ornate typefaces. The goal of your resume's design and typography is legibility. A successful resume design shows control over complex levels of information: headline, subheadline, location, bullet list, descriptions, captions, etc.

Resume Dos and Don'ts

DO include your personal branding in the design of your resume to show your design skills and understanding of typography, layout, color, scale, etc.

DO include your email address. Stick with a professional email address, such as MarySmith@email.com.

DO include your portfolio link.

DO create your resume in InDesign.

DO keep your resume to one page in length.

DO make multiple versions of your resume tailored to each job description and use keywords from the job description.

DO use professional convention when naming your resume file, such as MarySmith_HugeInc_Resume2018.pdf.

DO highlight your contributions to each role with action verbs.

DO use clear typographic hierarchy to create an easily-scanned flow to the information.

DO include your social media information to help employers find you on social media (LinkedIn, Twitter, Instagram).

DO test out a sample proof of your resume in color and black and white to check that everything looks good.

DO spell check your resume and ask someone else to review it before submitting it to potential employers.

DO your resume now, there is no reason to wait until graduation to work on your resume and portfolio.

DON'T use overly ornate typefaces and visuals.

DON'T overdesign your resume. The purpose of your design is to create legibility.

DON'T submit a resume created in Microsoft Word.

DON'T forget to include your involvement in design-related clubs, organizations, and any professional training you've received. This shows potential employers that you're committed to your design career and take initiative to grow professionally.

DON'T include your GPA. It's not required for designers.

DON'T include references, you can provide your references when asked.

DON'T forget to scrub your professional social media content before you provide them to potential employers. If you're concerned about specific content, make your account private.

DON'T let your resume get stale. Continually update your resume as you gain additional experience and develop new skills.

DON'T forget to compare your resume against your LinkedIn profile and fix any discrepancies. You want your resume and your LinkedIn profile to be completely in sync.

Top three tips for choosing the right typeface for your resume by Tim Sullivan, Designer at AREA 17

Tip 1: Convey your aesthetic.
With yourself as the client, your personal brand is your canvas to present your unfettered vision. Choose a typeface that embodies your aesthetic principles and communicates your personality as a designer. For example, the old-style serif-influenced Canela may convey that you imbue your work with classical elegance and flair, while the Modernist sans-derived Suisse Int'l may impart that you strip away ornament and let content speak for itself. As with any other brand, your personal brand needs to be distinguishable in a sea of competitors. Draw on your unique knowledge and taste to confidently express your own point of view.

Tip 2: Appeal to employers and clients.
By choosing a typeface that captures your design philosophy, you will be able to engage with your brand's target audience, which is the like-minded people you want to hire you. Whether you aim to join an agency, an in-house department, or practice independently, use your personal brand to attract your dream collaborators and let them know you speak the same visual language. Your choice of typeface is an integral component of what should be a thoroughly considered identity, since hiring managers and prospective clients will encounter your brand before assessing the work in your portfolio. If they recognize that you share a similar set of values, they will be able to envision a fruitful partnership.

Tip 3: Choose from quality collections.
Resumes are dense with information and require multiple levels of typographic hierarchy. To facilitate designing your resume, and to extend your brand to other touch points in print and on screens, choose a well-crafted typeface that is legible, robust, and flexible. In addition to learning the classics, be versed in the trending typefaces released by the prominent type designers of today. Below are a few of the highly regarded foundries the professional community turns to when selecting typefaces for personal and client projects. Ranging from behemoths to boutiques and mainstays to relative newcomers, the foundries on this list offer myriad quality typefaces from which to choose and thereby position yourself for success.

Recommended Type Foundries
- Colophon Foundry
- Commercial Type
- FontShop
- Grilli Type
- Hoefler & Co.
- Klim Type Foundry
- Lineto
- Linotype
- Monotype
- Optimo
- Swiss Typefaces
- TypeNetwork

Steer clear of over-designing. While it's perfectly fine to sparingly use elements such as illustration, color, infographics, and iconography on your resume, these visual elements should be minimal. Your resume's visual focus should be legibility, so concentrate on highlighting your contributions to the company without too many distractions. If you're going to use color, remember that your resume might be printed in black/white by your potential employer, so light colors like yellow or lime green may be illegible. Save your selfies for another use—a resume should not include your headshots.

Do a test. Print your resume in color and black and white to check how it will look in the hands of a potential employer.

The following pages show some ideas for resume layouts and formats. Industry professionals share their resume and talk about their process. You can also read the Tip corner to learn best practices in choosing and mixing the right typeface for your resume.

Resume Spotlight on. . .

Kevin Kan

Kevin Kan
Visual Designer
Google
New York, New York
google.com
callmekevin.com

Describe your process in designing your resume.

"My resume design process is pretty similar to most of the graphic design projects. There are four steps for the whole process:

1. Collect and organize the information I want to put in my resume. This is the most important step when I started to design my resume because it is such a limited space that I need to choose only the most valuable info. The info is usually more about who I am, when I graduated and started to work, what's my working experience, why I'm better than the other people.

2. Design. I always do research and collect inspirations on each design project, so does the resume design. Make sure you think broadly and don't narrow yourself into one or two specific concepts and style too soon. When I try a couple of options and put them together, my eye will have a clearer answer about which one fits me the best and which one can stand out for me. Software such as Photoshop, Illustrator, or InDesign are the standard tools for me to use on my resume design.

3. Media. Ten years ago, when I was a student in the design school, paper was the only platform for us to design for our resume. So we do care about the printing quality, color corrections, and paper materials we use. However, these days, when we design a resume, it's mostly for digital devices. What we consider now is more about format, size, legibility, visual experience, and accessibility.

4. The last, but not the least: double checking. Double check your copy, spelling, color correction, file settlement, file size, resolution, and so on. Make sure what you sent can be received and opened by other people."

Describe your process in creating your personal brand.

"When I started to create my personal brand, I always think about who I am and where I came from. Which areas I'm most interested in and what I want to do in the next 10 years. Figuring these out makes my personal style more unique and gives me clearer directions to do the explorations. I came from the South of China and got my Master's degree in New York. So for me, I have a really interesting culture mixing element to transfer to my own visual language to use in my website, logo, resume, and so on. I used red to combine with modern typographic to create Cultural Collision and Blend. This is my personal style and makes me stand out in millions of designers."

What's your advice to a young designer about designing their resume?

"When you design your resume, don't think about how to make it cool or unique on the style point. Because the style always changes. If you follow the trend, your resume will have no personality in it. A resume is more about storytelling and personality showing. If I show you a resume with all pink colors and a lot of illustration decoration, you can have a picture of the person in your mind even though you never meet me.

Think about yourself and find out your most shining personality and style. This could come from your regular life, the color of the clothing you like, the style of shoes you wear, the kind of books you read. Showing your real side to people through your resume is the most important part.

Then about resources, I encourage all of you to collect and prepare a resource library for yourself. You may find a designer's website which is interesting, you can find amazing graphics on a business magazine, or you may find a shopping website has really good interaction. You should collect all of these to be your own resource library for you to use anytime. I never narrow myself into any specific category or website, you can search 'Pinterest,' 'Design Inspirations,' 'Dribbble' to find inspirations, but it could also be 'ALDO,' 'MOMA,' 'Pentagram,' which can sometimes get you a surprise."

Resume Spotlight on. . .

Rudy Calderon

RUDY CALDERÓN
DESIGNER+PHOTOGRAPHER

rudy@rudycalderon.com
rudy.design
@rudycalderon

WHO AM I?

A self-motivated, problem-solver who is passionate about design and loves to work in a team environment. Sophisticated design sense, organized, and outgoing. An active adapter of latest design patterns and trends, able to manage and multi-task projects from ideation to completion.

SKILLS

SKILLS	FOCUS
Photoshop	Art Direction
Illustrator	Branding
InDesign	Corporate Identity
Dreamweaver	Photography
After Effects	Print Design
Wordpress	Typography
Microsoft Office	Editing

EDUCATION:

FARMINGDALE STATE COLLEGE 2013
Bachelor of Technology - Vis Com
Farmingdale State College Alumni
Award Winner 2013

SUFFOLK COMMUNITY COLLEGE 2009
AAS in Graphic Design

RECOGNITION:

FARMINGDALE STATE COLLEGE
Guest Lecturer
Spoke with the senior class about handling the pressures of Senior Project by giving tips on subjects such as time management and organizational skills that lead to success throughout the course.

ESOMANO PUPUSA SHOP
founder @esmano_nyc
Senior Thesis based on my Salvadoran heritage. Branding a resturant to be opened in NYC, highlighting El Salvador's rich culture in art and food. Developed a business plan and visual strategy for the brand through extensive research of other competitors and history of El Salvador.

EXPERIENCE

DISNEY STREAMING SERVICES, NEW YORK, NY MAY 19 – PRES
ART DIRECTOR, ESPN+
Ideate and implement design concepts, guidelines, and strategies in various digital marketing projects and oversee them to completion. Motivate and mentor visual, production and motion designers to help them use their talents effectively. Collaborate with design director and marketing teams to on-board client requirements. Revise content and presentations, approve/reject ideas, provide feedback to team.

MAJOR LEAGUE SOCCER, NEW YORK, NY MAR 16 – APR 19
DIGITAL DESIGNER
Support and maintain the design language of Major League Soccer websites (English & Spanish), social media and online campaigns. Art direct various creative and product photoshoots. Collaborating with marketing team members to uphold seasonal creative standards. Manage and art direct freelancers on various projects throughout the league season.

BROOKLYN NETS / BSE, BROOKLYN, NY JUN 14 – MAR 16
GRAPHIC DESIGNER
Creation and art direction of design elements that support and maintain the consistency of Barclays Center and Brooklyn Nets brands throughout the entire marketing spectrum (in print, online, e-mail marketing, in-arena, promotional products, direct mail, OOH vadvertising, etc.). Incorporating internal feedback, and collaborating with marketing team members to uphold creative standards.

WILEN NEW YORK, FARMINGDALE, NY JUN 13 – MAY 14
ASSISTANT ART DIRECTOR
Executing creative concepts that are on strategy across all direct response media, advertisments, and internal departments. Collaborate on concepts with senior members of the creative group. Organizing photoshoots & editing client work. Ensuring the continuity of the Wilen New York internal brand through all print and digitial communications.

CLIENTS INCLUDE › Verizon, TIME, SeriousFun, Pitney Bowes, Blink Fitness, Embrace Home Loans, and Metrocast Communications

CALDERON DESIGN + PHOTOGRAPHY MAR 11 – PRESENT
FREELANCE DESIGNER + PHOTOGRAPHER

CLIENTS INCLUDE › Miami Marlins, Complex Magazine, Hypebeast, Hypetrak, West NYC, American Outlaws Long Island Brooklyn Nets/Barclays Center & Core Leader NYC

MORE...

ADDITIONAL SKILLS: Strategic planning, budgeting, pre-press and production, Bilingual (English & Spanish)

INTERESTS: photography, biking, watching and playing soccer, keeping up with design & social media trends, and always on the endless pursuit to find the best Old Fashioned the Tri-State Area has to offer.

Rudy Calderon
Art Director, ESPN+
Disney Streaming Services
New York, New York
rudy.design

Describe your process in designing your resume.

"I start off by looking for my favorite typefaces. I have always like big, bold typefaces and I pair it with a legible body copy typeface. A great resource for pairing typefaces: typography.com.

Typefaces used here are:

- Integral CF by Connary Fagen Type Design
- Whitney by Hoefler & Co.

My design and typefaces have varied throughout the years. As I evolved as a designer, so did my choices in type. I usually mock-up a design in Illustrator before tidying it up and finalizing in InDesign. There you can set up character and paragraph styles which make updating your resume a breeze in the future."

Describe your process in creating your personal brand.

"This is an important part of becoming a designer. Whether you are getting a corporate job or full-time freelancing. You are promoting the most important thing—You. If you are not telling your story, no one else will.

1. Make a logo for yourself. Something that speaks to who you are. Use your favorite colors, typefaces. This will let prospective jobs and clients know who you are and possibly help you stand out among the rest.
2. Be consistent in your choices of colors, typefaces, and usernames on social media.
   You can't be ILuVDoGz on Twitter and @johnDoeDesigns on Instagram.
3. Share your work, collaborate with other designers, visit conferences and network."

What's your advice to a young designer about designing their resume?

"Share it with everyone, have them look over it. Show it to mom and dad, Joe at the pizza shop. Everyone. Let them write on it with corrections. It's not your last copy and it's never written in stone. Allow them to tell you what you can fix, and continually update it whenever you achieve something that you are proud of. It's your ticket to the dance, show up with your best stuff.

Have fun with it. You're a designer, not an accountant. Throw out the PowerPoint, don't even think about opening a Word doc, I'm serious. Let your creativity fly and make sure your resume stands out from the rest when the hiring manager receives it. If you notice your page starting to look too full, condense. You don't have to have that summer job you had at Target when you were 17.

If you've ever read a job description and said 'Hey, I can do that!' make sure you position your resume towards that job. Sprinkle some keywords, let the person reading your resume know that you know what job you're going to have if they decide to hire you.

I have a habit of going to the magazine stores weekly and spending about 20–30 minutes to myself, just looking at anything that catches my eye, always looking for interesting layouts and uses of color. It could be *Cosmopolitan* or *Forbes*. I'm always searching.

UnderConsideration
underconsideration.com

Brand New
https://www.underconsideration.com/brandnew
Corporate and brand identity. I found it very helpful in terms of what works and what doesn't when it comes to identity.

Art of the Menu
https://www.underconsideration.com/artofthemenu
Print trends, menu layouts from all over the world, color usage. Not your typical diner menus on this site.

My favorite inspiration site ever—**Quipsologies**
www.underconsideration.com/quipsologies
I've saved many links from this site alone.

FPO
www.underconsideration.com/fpo
Tons of resumes, business cards, card stock. If it's printed and it's really dope, it's on here.

Swissmiss
Swiss-miss.com
Has a cool weekly Friday link pack, just cool things that happen in the world, most related to design, some not."

123

Resume Spotlight on. . .

Jeffrey Betts

Describe your process in designing your resume.

"As I considered layouts for my resume I focused on creating a layout that has a clear structure and information hierarchy. After quickly sketching on potential layouts I decided to use a two column approach. Using this I was able to break out the types of information I was communicating. The left side has my education and skills background, whereas the right has my work experience. I set it up using Adobe InDesign with an underlying twelve column grid which helped me align and size the two main columns. I also included my logo and contact information at the top. You should aim to keep the resume to a single page. I chose to use typefaces that were readable and that were in my personal branding: Futura for headings and Proxima Nova for body copy."

Describe your process in creating your personal brand.

"I view a personal brand as an expression of you as a designer and your perspective on design and its purpose. For myself, I looked at my work as providing a means for people to better view and understand information, solve problems in their daily lives, and bring joy. You can also consider how you approach design tasks and projects—do you have a specific aesthetic or common theme throughout your work? My personal brand, as seen in much of my design work, is very minimalist and purposeful. It differentiates my work and communicates to others, including potential employers, who you are as a designer. For the visual aspects of your personal brand (typefaces, colors, illustrations, etc.), it may be helpful to look at other designers who you aspire to and how they developed their brand and other collateral."

What's your advice to a young designer about designing their resume?

"When designing your resume it is key that it is readable, legible, and effortless for the reader. Outside of your portfolio or website, it is your potential employer's first impression of your design strengths. Think about the elements that you are adding, what is their purpose, and if they help or hinder your design. For example, using a common resume trend, 'skills bars/charts,' usually do not provide enough information or context to the reader to be helpful in determining what skills you actually have. Often at times, these are seen as ways to fill space on the page.

Typography is equally as important as the layout. Consider the readability and legibility of the typefaces you choose and how they interact with one another. Consider writing the contents of your resume separately in an editor such as Google Docs, as the default spelling dictionary in Adobe InDesign is not as up to date as other tools are. Even with spell check, you should always read it over and proofread and not make needless typos.

There are also many resources available for resume design that showcase great examples. I recommend Bestfolios (bestfolios.com), where you can view portfolio website, case study, and resume design examples. For an accessible and well written piece on typography rules, I highly recommend referencing But-t-er-ick's Prac-ti-cal Ty-pog-ra-phy (practicaltypography.com). If you are looking for well-designed typefaces to use in your resume and branding, Adobe has recently made available thousands of fonts that are included with a Creative Cloud subscription. It is available on Adobe Fonts (formerly Typekit), and is licensed for unlimited desktop and web usage."

124

Jeffrey Betts
Product Designer

Elmont, NY | 516-316-4336 | www.linkedin.com/in/jeffreybetts
www.jeffreybetts.me | jeffrey@jeffreybetts.me

Technical Skills

- Photoshop
- Illustrator
- InDesign
- Dreamweaver
- Sketch
- Figma
- Axure RP
- InVision
- Zeplin
- MailChimp Development
- HTML/CSS and JavaScript

Additional Skills

- Strategic Planning
- Prototyping
- Technical Writing
- Budgeting and Estimating

Education

Bachelor of Technology, Visual Communications: Art & Graphic Design

State University of New York, Farmingdale State College

Experience

Founder, FOCA (focastock.com), Elmont, NY   **2014–Present**

Founded and developed a website with free photography for personal and commercial use under a CC0 license.

- Created and refined the core design framework and UI/UX for various components and page elements. FOCA has seen over 88,000 photo downloads and has had over 1,188,000 sessions since launch.
- Developed a custom Bootstrap-based WordPress theme that aligned with the design framework for rapid iteration, allowing for weekly content updates and an average of 2-3 feature updates per month.
- Established affiliate partnerships and monetization strategies for future growth.
- Managed social media pages and marketing efforts, with a combined reach of 2200 followers.

UI/UX Designer, Makr, Brooklyn, NY   **2013–2019**

Collaborated with CEO, Lead Product Designer, Art Director, Product Manager, Lead UI Architect on the cross-platform Makr product UI/UX (including a native iOS app and website), where users could create custom logos and printed products.

- Designed the logo creation and purchase experience in the Makr for iPad app. Incorporated new functionality that improved the editing experience and allowed for users to export their logo to use in other apps and services.
- Led the design and development of the Makr Help & Support website and in-app help integration. Met with product stakeholders to determine the information architecture and designed the user interface for the website and in-app components. Developed a custom WordPress theme with HTML/CSS and JS.
- Designed and implemented a data-informed update to the website's Shopify Cart page to better inform the user about their logo purchase, which over the course of several weeks resulted in an increase of conversion by 18%.
- Created wireframes and prototyped a refined internal Content Admin Tool in order to streamline uploading assets to the builder. Worked with the engineering team to identify an open-source framework and implement the changes, which enabled the Art Director to quickly upload, categorize, and sort assets.
- Sketched, drafted wireframes, prototyped, created specification documents, wrote user stories, exported assets, and articulated functionality requirements.

Graphic Design Intern, Warner Music Group, New York, NY   **2012**

Designed and produced various pieces, including promotional flyers, internal training documents, posters, Spotify covers, and email newsletters.

- Implemented a series of MailChimp newsletters with HTML/CSS and tested newsletters across different operating systems throughout the company.
- Participated on the Music Propaganda campaign, which seeks to curb music piracy across college campuses. Established a visual strategy, in collaboration with other design interns. Designed three posters, stickers, and online banners.

125

Jeffrey Betts
Experience Designer
Responsify
Brooklyn, NY
responsify.com
jeffreybetts.me

Resume Spotlight on. . .

Talia Brigneti

Describe your process in designing your resume.

"The ultimate goal for my resume was to arrive at something clean, simple, and easily digestible. I focused mainly on content layout and information architecture, primarily making sure that everything could fit in one page without over-cluttering it or leaving anything important out. The use of white space and playing with different font weights were critical in helping make the information easy to scan by creating interesting breaking points between each section. I chose Helvetica because this typeface offers a wide variation of font weights that allowed me to execute exactly as I intended. I also decided to use Illustrator to design my resume, since I wanted as much flexibility as possible aligning elements, such as tweaking spacing between sentences as well as individual letters. Once I had everything properly laid out, I included my logo and kept it as the only element of color on the page—I specifically wanted to draw attention to my name with the intention of making me (and my brand) memorable."

Describe your process in creating your personal brand.

"It took me many, many different revisions throughout the years to arrive at a brand that I truly identified with. I do not have a formal background in visual design, which is why branding was not something I was 'fluent' with. So I did what I always do when I need to accomplish something but don't know exactly how; I looked for inspiration both online and offline, I moved on to try many different variations, and asked for guidance from experts in the field.

The first thing that I focused on was coming up with my color palette and 'style.' In order to define my style, I examined a variety of things. For example, I considered the way I usually like to design products, the principles I stand by, the way I dress, and the type of art and environments that I'm inclined towards. This exercise immensely helped me to experiment with styles that felt compatible with my persona, which eventually landed me on a brand that truly speaks to the type of designer I am and the kind of work I love doing."

What's your advice to a young designer about designing their resume?

"Before jumping on to designing your resume, define the content first! Make sure you are communicating exactly what you have worked on, what you've accomplished across your projects/ventures and what skills you utilized for each of these. Highlight the skills and the work you are most proud of—you want to make sure your interviewer picks up on these if they are a good match for the role you're applying to. Brand yourself in a way that reflects your identity as a designer and that conveys your personality—don't be afraid to add a touch of quirkiness or humor if you feel like it, originality is good! Just don't overdo it. Last but not least, double check, triple check and check your spelling yet again, this may sound obvious, but too often it is overlooked, and a well written (and well designed) resume conveys professionalism and dedication."

126

Talia Brigneti | Experience Designer

Portfolio
www.talia.design

Work Experience

Google, Interaction Designer
May 2017 - Present | Mountain View, CA

Responsible for the UX & UI of products within the Ads organization. Ongoing work consists of designing richer ad formats for the Google Search page and Discover app, as well as systematic end-to-end experiences for emerging markets to drive monetization.

R/GA, Experience Designer
Jan 2015 - April 2017 | New York, NY

Defined information architecture and story for marketing websites, revamped eCommerce navigation flows to increase conversion, conceptualized campaigns end-to-end, and designed core UX for new apps. Leveraged tools such as prototyping, user journey analysis, and data visualization. Clients include Nike, Tiffany & Co, Google, and TD Bank.

Notable Projects:
- **Nike Commerce in the Cloud:** Consulted as embedded UX designer at Nike World Headquarters reshaping their online experience.
- **Google OnHub Website:** Defined structure, experience flow and digital interactions through storyboarding for the OnHub product launch website.

School Of Visual Arts, Teaching Assistant - Digital Design I
Sept 2016 - Present | New York, NY

Mentor students in design thought process, coordinate activities and define course goals.

Product Designer, Rexcise Technologies
Jul 2016 - Present | New York, NY

Developed MVP app design for early-stage startup in recreational sports industry.

AKQA, Creative Technology Intern
Sept - Dec 2014 | San Francisco, CA

Worked in 1 week sprints from concept to prototype utilizing 3D printing, augmented reality, and connected devices for clients such as DirecTV, Google, and Verizon.

Nottingham Spirk, Industrial Designe Intern
Jun - Sept 2013 | Cleveland, Ohio

Performed user research, product design, and prototype testing for a novel haircare appliance for Panasonic Healthcare.

Education

Savannah College of Art and Design   Class of '14, Magna Cum Laude
BFA in Industrial Design - Minors: Interaction Design, Service Design

Pontifical Catholic University of Peru (PUCP)   2009 - 2010
Art Foundations.

Skills

Pencil sketching and storyboarding to convey ideas and designs.
Market research, systematic design, usability testing.
Tools: Sketch, Principle, Adobe CC Suite, Solidworks. Familiar with HTML & CSS coding.

Honors & Mentions

Featured in renowned Peruvian magazine "Cosas" as notable professional abroad.   2017
Personal project "NUKE" featured on Core77 and Yanko Design blogs.   2014

127

Talia Brigneti
Interaction Designer
Google
San Francisco, California
google.com
Talia.design

Resume Spotlight on. . .

Lorenzo Iuculano

Lorenzo Iuculano
User Experience Designer

Lorenzoiuculano.com

EXPERIENCE	**User Experience Designer** October 2018 – Present *Think Company* Client consulting User experience strategy Onsite field researching	**Brand Architect** January 2017 – June 2017 *Vynleads* Developing concepts & strategies Developing brand voice & tone Overseeing digital products & content
	Freelance Designer May 2014 – Present *Possible Plausible* Creating brand identities and collateral Conducting research Product design	**Graphic Designer** August 2015 – January 2017 *Amana Tool* Solved UX problems Front end development Created digital and printed content
	Experience Designer June 2017 – August 2017 *Huge, Experience Design School* Exercised UX process Wireframing and prototyping Leveraged research and strategy	**Graphic Designer/Researcher** May 2014 – June 2015 *Bionic Solution* Created data visualizations Created prototypes for digital experiences Conducted market research for clients
EDUCATION	**Continuing Education** Visualizing Data, Summer 2015 *School of Visual Arts, Manhattan, NY*	**Bachelor of Technology** Visual Communications 2014 *Farmingdale State College, Farmingdale, NY* Latin Honors: Cum Laude [3.6gpa]

NOTE-WORTHY

State Finalist for Dare to Risk Entrepreneurship Grant
New York State Business Plan Competition

Finalist for National Educational Alumni Grant

Nominated for SUNY's Undergraduate Research Symposium

Featured on AIGA Portfolios

Represented Farmingdale State College
at the Student Art Exhibition: Albany

Lorenzo Iuculano
User Experience Designer
Think Company
Philadelphia, Pennsylvania
thinkcompany.com
Lorenzoiuculano.com

Describe your process in designing your resume.

"My process starts with thinking about who will be reading my resume. Typically a person is going to be going scanning over a resume pretty quick, so I have to decide what is the most important and relevant information for that person. I ask myself 'What does this person care about, and what do they want to know?' I try to put myself in the hiring manager's shoes and apply what they are looking for to what I can offer.

I open up InDesign and immediately make a grid. I prefer InDesign because it is designed for publishing and typesetting. You can use a wrench to hammer a nail, but why would you?

For typefaces I use Adelle and Adelle-Sans. I like these because they are a natural pairing and have a few styles to help organize and create scannable hierarchy. Adelle-Sans is used to guide the reader in section titles like EXPERIENCE, EDUCATION, NOTEWORTHY. Adelle is used for all the content. Using the sans-serif for framing, and serif for content helps to create a nice division. I make my content more scannable by using the typography and leaving plenty of space. I would stick to 1-2 typefaces, and if I pair 2 typefaces, I like them to have good contrast.

When I think I'm done, I'll print it out and read it. There are going to be things you noticed on the printed page that are difficult to see on screen. I had a hard time putting together my initial resume, and it took many iterations over many years to get to something I was happy with. However, that doesn't mean I'm done, this is something that will constantly evolve with me through my career."

Describe your process in creating your personal brand.

"The best advice I ever got was brand what's different. I didn't do that. Like anything you do where you have to look at yourself critically, it's difficult. Like lots of my classmates, I just kept playing with my initials until I made something that looked cool enough. Are my initials the most unique and different thing about me? I hope not.

If I were to rebrand I would look at myself critically and ask the following questions: What is unique about me? What are my differentiating traits? Who do I want to become? I would come up with a few keywords. I'd use those words to write an interesting statement or paragraph, and I would sketch off of that.

To me, brands are living things. I haven't rebranded myself because sometimes a brand can grown or change, gain new meaning, or age not so well. In the case of my brand, it's an okay mark and has the look and feel of someone who might be a designer. I've kept it because reminds me where I started from, as a student with no process, and how much I've grown since then. At the time it represented nothing, but today it represents an artifact of someone who is willing to look back, be critical of their own work, and learn. I've owned that mistake."

What's your advice to a young designer about designing their resume?

"Creating a resume is a design challenge because it is an opportunity to display three important qualities, attention to detail, typography, and sense of design.

It's always difficult to write about yourself. Especially if you're like me and have worked a not so glamorous jobs. You may feel like that job was providing no value to your career. However, everything has some value. It's important to be optimistic and look at things in a positive light. There will be skills in any job that will be translatable to your goal.

When writing any content, the best advice I can give is to write down anything, don't put a lot of stock in your first draft. It's important to get something on the page, you can always go back and edit.

Good practice for resumes and cover letters is to reference the specific job you're applying to and directly address their needs with your skills. It's important to not undersell yourself. You have experience, write it confidently.

Check out Ellen Lupton's *Thinking with Type* for grid basics and sizing your type, and *Bird by Bird: Some Instructions on Writing and Life* by Anne Lamott for writing."

Resume Spotlight on. . .

Lori Weiss

Describe your process in designing your resume.

"For my resume design, my goal was for it to look professional and easy to read, but still portray myself creatively as a designer. I relied on grids and typography to set up a clean foundation and then decorated the content using my color palette for my personal brand. In Adobe InDesign, I set up my document with a grid and also made sure to include a baseline grid so all the text is aligned horizontally across columns. Setting a tight baseline grid will make your text look clean, professional, and easy to read. To create typographic hierarchy and contrast, I chose a typeface that had a variety of weights I could leverage to emphasize different pieces of content. To further create distinction and contrast I used my brand color to make section headers stand out. Lastly, I printed my resume on paper to proofread and check it for good readability."

Describe your process in creating your personal brand.

"A personal logo is our opportunity as designers to give a potential employer a glimpse at our brand identity skills and our unique personality. For me, hand-lettering is something I love to do, so it felt natural for me to create a hand-drawn logo using the first letter of my name. My logo showcases my custom letter design and also my ability to create vector art in Illustrator.

Try to see how far your own initials can take you. You might get a lucky combination of letters that pair nicely together or even create a ligature! If there is an opportunity to show off a unique skillset too with your personal identity, take advantage of that."

What's your advice to a young designer about designing their resume?

"My advice to young designers is to always remember that your resume is a living document and will evolve as you grow and add experiences. I look back at my first resume and cringe at how it looked, but at the time, it landed me my first design job, meaning someone still saw potential in me through it. Being a designer, it is so easy to get caught up in the pressure to have a 'perfect' resume but you don't want to analyze it to the point where an opportunity passes. You trade in your resume for a job, and that job will give you back a new experience to add to your resume, and you'll continuously grow.

In terms of resume content, one thing I want to stress is the importance of matching your skills to the job posting, and don't be afraid to show your progress to others and ask for advice.

Thinking ahead to the job interview phase, sometimes you may be asked to interview in a panel format which means you'll need to have several printed copies of your resume to hand out. Keep in mind that color backgrounds can use a lot of ink and are generally harder on the eyes to read.

When I need visual inspiration, I like to look at the resumes of professionals in positions that I aspire to be in. LinkedIn is a good tool to find people and browse through their online portfolios. The Dribble community is a good place to look for eye candy, as well as Behance. Despite all the resources out there, always be authentic and true to yourself."

Lori Weiss

Visual designer for print, web, mobile, and AR/VR.

Contact Me

WEBSITE .... lorianneweiss.com

Skills

DESIGN

Wireframing
Prototyping
Information architecture
Site maps
Personas
Usability testing
Hand-lettering
Illustration
Calligraphy
AR/VR UI Design

SOFTWARE + TOOLS

Adobe Creative Suite
Sketch
InVision
Zeplin
Unity
Microsoft Office
MicroStrategy
Tableau
HTML5/CSS3/jQuery
Wordpress

BUSINESS ANALYSIS

Requirements documentation
Test case writing
Quality assurance testing

Certifications

Tableau

Sales Accreditation For Partners, December 2016.

MicroStrategy

Certified Dashboard and Mobile Developer, September 2015.

Work Experience

Deloitte Digital

New York, NY | Visual Designer | September 2017—Present

- Connect with clients to align their business needs with technology solutions.
- Work closely with cross-functional teams on projects varying from mobile applications and websites to immersive virtual and augmented reality experiences.
- Create user interface designs that are on brand for clients and follow the project's creative vision and overall business strategy.
- Apply knowledge of UI/UX to immersive experience design.

Data Meaning Services Group

Tyson's Corner, VA | UX Design Associate | July 2015—August 2017

- Designed mobile and web applications for both internal and client projects.
- Consulted clients on best UI/UX practices and oversaw design implementation.
- Contributed to meetings throughout project lifecycle by participating in discovery sessions, scrum meetings, and review sessions.
- Collaborated and communicated with UX team, software developers, and project managers in order to ensure successful execution and delivery of projects.
- Presented and recorded educational videos for Data Meaning's YouTube channel.

Whole Foods Market

Manhasset, NY | Store Graphic Artist | May 2014—June 2015

- Designed and created illustrated chalk boards, computer generated graphics, and signage for the Manhasset store following brand standards and seasonal toolkits.
- Maintained high standard of visual quality and consistency throughout departments.
- Collaborated with Team Leaders to assure all sales and marketing objectives were met for each department and the overall store.

Speaking Engagements

SUNY Undergraduate Research Conference

Brockport, NY | Student Presenter | April 2015

- Represented Farmingdale State College in a state-wide research symposium.
- Presented user research and prototype of the iPad App "Xheight."

School of Visual Arts

New York, NY | Guest Lecturer | March 2015

- Prepared a lesson and led a hand-lettering workshop for 19 students in the undergraduate course, "What's Your Type."

Education

Farmingdale State College

Visual Communications: Art + Graphic Design
Bachelor of Technology, Cum Laude, May 2015.

Lori Weiss
Visual Designer
Deloitte Digital
New York, New York
deloittedigital.com
lorianneweiss.com

Resume Spotlight on. . .

Tadeu Magalhães

Describe your process in designing your resume.

"When I design my resume, as with any editorial piece, I prefer using Adobe InDesign as it gives me more control over typography, grids and other elements. It is really helpful for me to approach it as an editorial project: I start by setting up the grid and choosing a font that is elegant and easy to read.

For the font sizes, I tend to use one or two sizes at the most, to avoid creating a busy design, and focus on using other visual elements to create hierarchy such as spacing, key lines, etc. Given the functional nature of a resume, it is really important that all the information is organized in a very clear and straightforward manner, and all in one page if possible. For this reason, I avoid using quirky elements, unnecessary illustrations or typography that is distracting. The goal is for the reader to have a quick glance at my professional and academic experience, as well as recognition and awards. The easier I make it for a recruiter to find that information, the more successful the resume will be."

Describe your process in creating your personal brand.

"Creating a personal brand for ourselves can be tricky. It is important to let the work we are presenting as designers to speak for itself. A designer's personal brand should be a platform to display the work we create for clients—not a distraction from it. Keep it simple and focus on the client work you are presenting. Make sure the elements you create for your brand are highlighting the client work, not competing with it. This applies to the font we choose, colors and how we set up the page layouts."

What's your advice to a young designer about designing their resume?

"Focus on including only information that is relevant for the job you are applying for, and remove anything that is filler. It is tempting to include personal bits to lighten up the resume and give it character, but these rarely contribute to the decision to bring you in for an interview. In reality, they often create the opposite effect. Choose a font that is clean and elegant. This will convey confidence and your grasp of typography and grid systems."

132

Tadeu Magalhães

+ 1 646 714 ██████

tadeumagalhaes.com

Experience

2016 – Present
Senior Art Director
Huge

2009 – 2016
Design Director
RoAndCo

2007 – 2009
Art Director & Senior Designer
Agência Dez (Brazil)

2004 – 2007
Freelance Designer
Coletivo Contorno (Brazil)

2005
Freelance Designer
Ogilvy & Mather (Brazil)

2004
Freelance Designer
Voltz Design (Brazil)

Education & Skills

B.A., Graphic Design and Visual Communication, 2007
Universidade do Estado de Minas Gerais (UEMG)
Belo Horizonte MG, Brazil

Broad knowledge of print production, print methods and materials, and web design. Highly skilled on the Adobe Creative Suite, including Photoshop, Illustrator, InDesign, Acrobat; HTML, CSS, and WordPress.

Awards

2013
FPO Awards – Radical Production Award, Judges' Pick

2012
FPO Awards
Brand New Awards
Print Regional Awards

2011
FPO Awards – Best of Category Mix
Brand New Awards
Communication Arts Annual 2010

Speaking Engagements

2014
How Design Live - The Dieline Conference
May 14th - Boston, MA
Fashion Branding: From Inspiration to Packaging

Features

Big Brand Theory
Published by Sandu, 2012

Mini Graphics 2
Published by Sandu, 2012

Not For Sale – For Promo Only
Published by Viction:ary, 2011

By Invitation Only
Published by Viction:ary, 2010

133

Tadeu Magalhães
Senior Art Director
HUGE
Brooklyn, New York
hugeinc.com
tadeumagalhaes.com

Resume Spotlight on. . .

Ilgin Sezer

Describe your process in designing your resume.

"After going through many different iterations and trying out a few different quirky formats (hello infographic resume), I landed with this simple design that I felt was more true to my nature. I wanted to make it easily scannable, so I designated areas on the page for the main content, dates, and supporting skill sets, and established a clear type hierarchy. I opted out of any visual frills on the resume; I think the place to display those design chops is the work sample."

Describe your process in creating your personal brand.

"I've always liked the idea of having a simple and easily identifiable mark. I enjoy clean modern lines, so when it was time to create my brand, a monogram stamp was the way to go for me. To accompany the mark, I picked the quiet confidence of Calibre. It puts a modern twist to a familiar Grotesk flavor, and is a typeface I won't easily get tired of looking at."

What's your advice to a young designer about designing their resume?

"Understand your audience, and if necessary, have a few different versions of your resume to emphasize different skill sets. Let the content and style be determined by who you're sending the resume to.

It's ok to be high level, as long as you define a career path. Resume is like a teaser. It's supposed to get people interested to hear more. Details can be revealed during the interview."

Ilgın Sezer

ilginsezer.com

Professional Experience

17 - Present

Huge, Associate Creative Director / New York NY
Create future forward brand experiences across industries that define how customers interact with digital products and services. Manage design in collaboration with product, UX and technology teams on high profile accounts. Contribute to $5M/yr new business growth. Set teams up for success by evolving internal processes. Partner with other discipline leadership to ensure a happy, challenged, and productive team.

16 - 17

DigitasLBi, Creative Lead / New York NY
Envisioned how digital products in the enterprise can yield better user experiences and brought the vision to life through design solutions that inspire and excite. Worked closely with clients and agency partners to define brand expression. Partnered with creative engineers and copywriters to conceptualize and execute activations for integrated, cross-channel initiatives.

14 - 16

VSA Partners, Senior Designer / New York NY
Applied design thinking to bring consumer-quality design to the enterprise. Served as design lead on multiple projects using Agile Scrum methodology. Work includes a variety of IBM products built to streamline its internal communication channels such as BluePages—IBM's professional networking service, and yourIBM—a cognitive dashboard for IBM employees.

12 - 14

Infinia Group, Design Associate / New York NY
Led creative process on various interactive design projects and provided quality assurance in implementation. Created print and digital communications for clients including Mount Sinai Hospital and BNP Paribas.

10 - 12

Darling Agency, Designer / New York NY
Designed branding, print and interactive solutions. Took part in every step of the creative process from developing concepts to presenting final work.

Education

13 - 14

Cooper Union / New York NY
Postgraduate Certificate in Typeface Design
Studied digital typeface design and lettering principles, with a focus on technique, history and theory.

08 - 09

London College of Communication / London UK
Postgraduate Diploma in Design for Visual Communication
Elected Course Representative, completed the course as first in class.

03 - 07

Oberlin College / Oberlin OH
Bachelor of Arts Degree, double major in Studio Arts and Cinema Studies, High Honors. Received Oberlin College International Scholarship for four academic years. Recipient of Coluccio Salutati Award for outstanding academic achievement while attending Syracuse University Studio Arts program in Florence, Italy.

Skills

Software
AfterEffects
CSS
Figma
HTML
Illustrator
InDesign
Invision
Photoshop
Principle
Robofont
Sketch

Technical
Bookbinding
Letterpress
Screen printing

Language
German (basic)
Italian (basic)
Turkish (native)

135

Ilgin Sezer
Associate Creative Director
Huge
New York, New York
hugeinc.com
ilginsezer.com

Cover letter clinic

When you're applying for jobs, you'll want to stand out with a tailored cover letter. A good cover letter gives a potential employer a glimpse into your personality, your strengths and why you're interested in the company and the role. The content of your cover letter should be concise and direct (three paragraphs is a good general length of a cover letter). A great cover letter should inspire the reader to want to see your resume or even call you the same day.

Know your audience:

Don't just copy and paste the same cover letter from company to company. Take the time to write tailored cover letters that show your understanding of the company, the job description, how you're a perfect fit for the role, and why.

Get personal:

Address your cover to a specific name. Don't address it to "Whom it may concern," or "Dear Sir or Madam." Use LinkedIn to find out the name of the recruiter who's leading the search, or the name of the hiring manager, or the creative director.

Design your cover letter:

Just like you've designed your resume, use the same grid, colors, and branding on your cover letter to show consistent visual language of your personal brand. Remember to include your contact information on your cover letter.

Finally, make it easy for the company to find your resume by naming it YourName_CoverLetter.pdf

Mistakes that will get your cover letter ignored:

- Writing a generic cover letter
- Writing a "me" centric cover letter
- Writing a long, rambling cover letter
- Submitting a cover letter with spelling errors
- Mistakenly writing the wrong company name or the wrong job
- Misspelling the person's or the company's name

136

How to write the perfect cover letter

Your cover letter should focus on the potential employer, not yourself. The perfect cover letter tells how you can make a difference in the company based on your skills and experience. Instead of writing detailed paragraphs about all your accomplishments, show a genuine interest in the company and the specific role, and prove that you're the right person to help.

Keep it short:
The hiring manager will probably spend 10–20 seconds reading your cover letter, so you want to be succinct. Three paragraphs is the ideal length.

Paragraph 1: Introduce yourself
Use a hook in your first sentence to engage the reader. Don't start your cover letter with the dreadfully boring, "I am writing to apply for the position of. . ." Instead, think of how you can pitch yourself with a hook. Did you visit the company during a school field trip and fall in love with it? Or perhaps you attended a design event, where you were inspired by the work of speaker, who happened to be a creative director at the company.

Paragraph 2: The meat
Read the job description and pick 2–3 qualifications or requirements that match your own experience and skills. Use this paragraph to demonstrate that you have these qualifications or skills, by giving specific examples of how, when, and where you've used them.

Tailor your cover letter to the specific company and job description. Don't just re-write your resume, instead emphasize the skills that align with the role. You may want to include class assignments, personal projects, or professional responsibilities that illustrate your expertise in the areas the hiring manager is looking for.

You can write about one experience in-depth, or use a couple of shorter experiences to demonstrate relevant experiences.

Paragraph 3: Wrap up
Reiterate your interest in the company and the role. Provide your contact information and your portfolio URL, and sign off!

Your cover letter will be structured something like this:

Dear Marissa,

The first time I visited [Company], I was on a school trip with my undergraduate design program. I remember feeling inspired by the work with [Client]. My passion for product design, user experience, apps, and my experience in digital make me an ideal candidate. When I learned that [Company] is hiring a Junior Designer, this was a perfect opportunity for me to apply and contribute to a company who believes in delighting the user with seamless user experience.

I interned as a product design intern at [Company], a digital ad agency in Summer 2017, as a part of the [name of the team or project], helping to launch a new responsive website. I gained the experience in collaborating with other designers, as well as engineers, copywriters, and strategists. Through my previous design internship, I learned how to be a team player: interacting with people of various interests and backgrounds, and confidently sharing my thoughts to fellow team members.

I believe that digital design can connect with users' emotions through the interaction between technology and us. Additionally, I am the Editor of my university's design blog, where I contribute weekly articles. I want to work at [Company] because I am inspired to learn that [Company] publishes regular design articles on Medium. I live and breathe design, and I am confident that I can make a difference at [Company].

Please see the attached resume for my qualifications. Additionally, my portfolio can be viewed at [URL].

I look forward to speaking with you. I can be reached at [phone number] and [email]. Thank you for your time and consideration.

Sincerely,

[Your name]

ALSO! Don't forget: Proofread, and get a second pair of eyes!

Nothing kills your chance at getting hired like a typo, grammar mistake, misspelling, or an incorrect spelling of the hiring manager's name. Proofread, proofread, proofread, and then ask a friend to review your materials one more time.

Interview clinic

Ok, you made it! You finished your portfolio, wrote and designed your resume and cover letter, and applied for that dream job. Finally, you check your email, and the recruiter from your dream job reached out for a phone screen. What's a phone screen? What do you do? How do you prepare?

The hiring process

Generally, the design hiring process consists of 3 steps:

Step 1: The phone screen where you'll talk to the recruiter to see if you're a good match.

Step 2: On-site interview where you'll interview with members of the team and get assigned a design exercise (if you move forward).

Step 3: Final on-site interview where you might be asked to present your design exercise and meet with key hiring decision makers.

Step 1: The phone screen

Recruiters sort through hundreds of applicants' materials daily. Once you're flagged as a good match (i.e., your resume shows relevant experience, cover letter is personal and tells a story of why you're a good match, and your book shows relevant work), you'll be invited to have a quick phone screen with the recruiter.

This is an opportunity for the recruiter to find out more about you, hear your elevator speech and hear how you talk about your work, ask basic questions, and then make a decision on whether or not to bring you in for an on-site interview where you'd meet the team.

The phone screen might begin with the recruiter explaining the job description and the ideal candidate, and then asking you some basic questions:

Tell me about yourself.

What do you know about our company?

Can you walk me through your work?

What's your favorite project and why?

Why are you interested in this role? In our company?

Where do you currently work? Or tell me about your most recent summer internship. What did you do there? Who was on your team? What project are you proud of?

What compensation are you expecting?

Do you have any questions?

The phone screen is important because you want to show the recruiter that you're a good match for the role and they should bring you on-site to meet the actual project team.

Take time to prepare for the phone screen so you can move forward and be invited to the on-site interview. Begin by researching the company's website and their portfolio of work. Follow the company on social media (Facebook, Instagram, Twitter, LinkedIn) to get an understanding of their culture, recent projects, main clients, office events, community involvement, quirks, etc. Read the job description again and make sure you understand what they're looking for in the candidate.

Go on LinkedIn and find out more background information on the recruiter who'll be interviewing you. You might find that you went to the same university, or have a connection in common, which will be a great way to break the ice.

Schedule the phone screen at a time where you can be in a quiet place, with zero distractions, with your portfolio, resume and cover letter, and the job description in front of you, so you can quickly reference something, in case it comes up in conversation. Never take the phone screen while you're driving or at a loud coffee shop where you might be distracted or have poor phone reception. Be prepared and professional with first impressions.

Have a notepad ready so you can take notes during the phone screen, and pour yourself a glass of water (you might want something stronger after the interview!).

Have bullets of what you're going to say during the phone screen. Also, have a list of questions you want to ask the recruiter. Ask lots of questions throughout the phone screen, don't just save all your questions to the end.

Stay calm. If you're nervous, do something to calm down, like yoga stretches, meditation, or listen to your favorite music.

Step 2: On-site interview

Hooray! You passed the phone screen. The recruiter would like to bring you in for an on-site interview to meet the team. The on-site interview is an opportunity for you to meet key hiring decision makers and (if you move forward in the interview process), you might be assigned a design exercise.

6 points on interviewing
By Sean King, Senior Web Designer, PVH Corp

I've been a working designer for over 20 years. I've reviewed lots of books, and interviewed, hired, and managed a few new designers. Here are a few thoughts and observations on successfully interviewing for a design job.

1. For every design internship and entry-level job I ever listed, I got 50–100 resumes. I usually met with at least 10 candidates in person. It isn't necessarily about you. You could be a great candidate, there could simply be someone better for that job. What does this mean to you? Don't beat yourself up about not being the best person for a job out of 100 or more applicants. Just try again.

2. With that many candidates for one job, I had to just mercilessly cull the list. As soon as I saw a typo in a resume or website or portfolio, they were off the list. If their resume wasn't designed well, off the list. If their resume wasn't legible or had a confusing hierarchy, off the list. If their web portfolio was hard to find, or contact info was hard to find, off the list. What does this mean to you? Make your resume beautiful and flawless. Get someone else to critique it and proofread it, and get a second person to proofread it again.

3. When I had culled the list into meetings, I expected them to show up on time, be polite, dress decently, have a great book, and present their work well. I saw some great designs that were mocked up very poorly—craftsmanship counts. What does this mean to you? Make your portfolio flawless. Dress to impress. Make sure you know how to get to the office. Maybe do a practice run before the interview.

4. I also saw lots of portfolios that were paper versions of the web or PDF portfolios. The impressive candidates brought something extra when they met me. It might be a 3D mockup of one or two pieces, it might be a sample of actual produced work. What does this mean to you? If you have the interview, you haven't damned yourself yet. Now impress them. Show them more than they could see online.

5. No matter how good their student work was, I weighed actual client work far more heavily. I know you didn't have a perfect brief, or careful attention of an instructor, or even very much time, to do that client work. That's why I'm more interested in it. I want to know that you can produce good work under pressure, and deal with all the compromises real client work demands. What does this mean to you? Include real client work. If you don't have any, get some. Take the best job you can actually get. Don't hold out to work for Stefan Sagmeister if he isn't offering you a job. It could be a nonprofit or community organization. It could be your school's newspaper. Show them something that isn't just an assigned class project.

6. I met many new designers with a chip on their shoulder. When you are starting out, that design degree is just the beginning of your education. It takes a lot of work to manage a new inexperienced designer, the manager is signing up to be 40% teacher and 60% manager, and still get their own work done somehow. Someone who seemed like a know it all or very needy did not make the cut. What does this mean to you? Do everything you can to show how attentive and helpful you can be. Make it easy to schedule the interview. Make it easy to reschedule if they need to. If they have comments on your book, listen. Better yet, write them down. Come prepared with questions about the job, and write down the answers.

Keep your chin up. Work on improving that book and website every day. Good luck.

140

4 tips for design presentations
by Rietje Becker, Creative Director at Soulsight

Tip 1: Prepare

Prior to the meeting, take some time to review the designs you intend to share. Identify what makes your designs compelling, and how they answer the brief. Present the idea, not the minutiae. Take notes. It is not important to remember what you wrote down word-by-word. You want to sound natural, and not overly rehearsed. Time yourself—don't spend too long on each concept.

Tip 2: Relax and be yourself.

Confidence in yourself and your work is critical if you want people to value the work you are presenting. You can't expect your audience to believe in your work if you don't appear to believe in it yourself. When you can, and it seems appropriate, make jokes. Be yourself. This will help them to lower their guard, and keeps their attention. Make sure you make eye contact while you're presenting.

Tip 3: Identify your bad habits

These are things you may not realize you are doing. To identify them, record yourself or ask a friend or colleague to watch you do a test presentation.

Look out for:

Uh, um, sort of, kind of, and like:
These are things that are said often, and can distract your audience. Challenge yourself to pause instead. You don't have to fill each second with speech.

Nervousness:
People often get nervous. The more presentations you'll do, the more comfortable you will be.

Loss of voice (nervous reaction):
If you find this is an issue for you, keep a cup of water near you, but watch your gesturing.

Fidgety hands, speaking too softly, looking down, looking at the designs/not the audience, rambling:
Once you are aware you do these things it is easier to stop.

Tip 4: DOs and DON'Ts

Do fluctuate the tone of your voice as you present to place emphasis on important parts of your presentation.

Do use key words/phrases. In most cases clients need to sell their preferred designs to their supervisors. Make it easy for them by presenting simply and using language that will be compelling to them to use themselves. Key words/phrases can be descriptive terms for a design, concept names, etc. You'll know you've communicated them successfully if you hear them repeated them back to you during their feedback. It may help to change your tone, or pause before or after, to stress the phrase.

Do use language from the project brief to support your designs.

Don't try to use words you don't know or fully understand. You don't need to have an extensive vocabulary to be a good presenter.

Do use your intuition. When you feel like your audience is getting bored—eyes straying, checking of phones, etc.—speed up your presentation. If you are standing, move to a different part of the room or change the tone of your voice. Present the following sentence more enthusiastically. You are likely taking too long to present your ideas.

If your presentation is on screen don't look at it and read the slides. Summarize what's on the pages. Never turn your back on the client. Stand to the side of the screen so you can gesture to it if needed, but do not block it. If the presentation is printed similar rules apply.

If you are presenting print outs, always take the time to ensure the order is right prior to the meeting. If you can, cover them up so that you can 'reveal' them one-at-a-time.

If you are presenting as part of a team, do plan roles in advance.

Do keep abbreviated presentation notes in an open notebook near where you are presenting, just in case you lose track of your thoughts.

What should you do? How do you prepare? You might feel nervous, so take a deep breath. You've got this. Remember, an interview is as much you interviewing the company to make sure the company is the right fit for you, as it is them making sure you're the right fit for them.

First impressions are important, so be aware of how you interact with everyone you come in contact with, including the security guard, front desk receptionist, recruitment coordinators, as well as the creative directors and the project interview team.

You may be asked similar questions as you were asked during the phone screen. However, the main difference is you're now speaking with the project team that will be your teammates. So your answers can be more in-depth than when you were speaking with the recruiter during the phone screen.

Tell me about yourself.

Can you walk me through your work?

What's your favorite project and why?

Why are you interested in this role? In our company?

What are you hoping to learn?

Where do you currently work? Or tell me about your most recent summer internship. What did you do there? Who was on your team? What project are you proud of?

What is an example of a conflict or a challenges you've encountered and how did you deal with it?

Can you give me an example where you took initiative on a project?

Explain your creative process as a designer.

What is your favorite digital product or app and why?

What is your favorite campaign out there, and why?

Do you have any questions?

Step 3: Final on-site interview where you might be asked to present your design exercise

If you made it through the previous round, you might be assigned a design exercise. This might be a fictitious client and your ask may be given a design brief, and assigned to design a solution.

What's a design exercise?
Employers want to see how you think, and how you sell your work. A design exercise is a chance for potential employers to see how you think about solving problems, and how you defend your work. For example, design a mobile app (3 key screens) that appeals to millennials to find volunteer opportunities in New York City, or re-imagine a compelling homepage and story page for a popular newspaper site that targets how today's users are consuming and sharing news content.

You'll then be invited to a final on-site interview to present your solution to the group. There might be a break after your presentation, followed by final one-on-one interviews with additional members of the team.

Document your process
When you're given a design brief for your design exercise, read it carefully and ask of questions before you get started. Get clarity on what you need to do. Then, approach the exercise as you would any project—find out information about what you're doing, who it's for, how it will be used/experienced/read, what you're trying to achieve, what is the brand of the "client," and what are the constraints of the final execution.

Create moodboards, take pictures of your initial sketches, document any user research notes you've done to arrive at your final solution, include project artifacts that support your final solution such as wireframes, user journeys, diagrams, etc. You'll want to share your thinking in the final presentation.

Tell a story, not just a presentation
Think about your design exercise as a story, not just a presentation of your solution. Include your process in your final presentation. Typically, you'll be able to bring your laptop and project your final presentation in the interview. Most candidates design the presentation that includes the background of the exercise, research, pictures of initial sketches, moodboards, and final work.

Keep your presentation to 15–20 minutes to allow room for questions from the interviewers.

You can stand out by going above and beyond the initial ask. For example, if the design exercise is asking for you to design an activity screen for a fitness app, you might want to also show the team how you imagine the home screen, or you might want to show how this fitness app can be marketed through a campaign. Note: you should only do extra work if (and only if) your actual design exercise is 100% complete.

141

Interview tips
By Sean King, Senior Web Designer, PVH Corp

Before the interview:

Use your contacts. People look for designers recommended by someone they trust. Share your resume with professors, coworkers, former employers, and anyone else who might be able to pass it along to someone who needs help.

Be friendly and make it easy to meet. Work with the person interviewing you to find a time that works for them. They need to hire someone to help them, and this is your first opportunity to show how helpful you can be.

Be flexible. The job market is very tough right now. The best strategy for someone starting out is to take the best job you can actually find and use that experience to work towards your ideal job.

Research the company. Learn something about their clients and their work. If you have any questions about them, write them down and bring that list of questions. If they have done some work you admire, write that down and mention it.

Edit your resume. Keep it current, make it clear, and make sure your spelling and punctuation are correct. Have someone else proofread it for you.

Edit your portfolio. 8–12 pieces is a good rule of thumb, but don't include anything that isn't your best work. 6 awesome pieces is better than 6 great ones and 4 more mediocre ones. Make sure the craftsmanship of your portfolio and samples is top-notch. This is not the time for "good enough."

During the interview:

Arrive 5 minutes early. If you are earlier, go get a coffee somewhere nearby.

Dress nicely. A rule of thumb is to dress a step or two better than you expect to on the job. Design firms usually have a relaxed dress code, so you probably won't need to wear a suit. No short skirts, old t-shirts, ripped jeans, or low cut shirts. Dressing well shows that you care about the job, and that you can present yourself professionally.

Have a conversation, not a monologue. Interviewers are looking for your ability to speak intelligently about your work. They are also hoping to learn about your real personality and interests, so be yourself. Paradoxically, they easiest way to learn to speak conversationally about your work is to practice presenting it.

Always be confident, enthusiastic, and express a willingness to learn. Remember that art school is just the beginning of your design education.

Remember that an interview is a two-way street. While presenting yourself, also make sure it is a place you want to work. Ask questions about the company and their work. (Remember your list!)

Every interview can be a learning experience. If you learn something, then it is worth your time. Remembering this can help you stay calm during the interview.

After the interview:

Send a thank you note or email. The interviewer has taken precious time to meet with you, thank them for the opportunity they have given you.

Interviewing DOs and DON'Ts
by Rietje Becker, Creative Director at Soulsight

Usually your interviewer already knows what your work looks like from your website or portfolio show. The interview is about getting to know you.

Do make sure you come across as interested and attentive. Sit up in your chair, listen to what your interviewers are saying, remember their names and ask them questions. Always be confident, enthusiastic, and express a willingness to learn.

At the onset of the interview, give them your resume to review. Do make sure you bring enough for all attendees.

Do research the company and potential job position. Appearing informed on previous work the agency has done and relevant industry news will show them that you came prepared and can take initiative. Employers will often question candidates about this, as well.

Do consider your outfit. Designers are generally given a lot of leeway, but try to avoid anything distracting or too casual (holes, obvious stains, etc.).

Don't be late. Plan the night before, have your clothes and portfolio ready. Map out your travel efficiently, so that you will arrive early. Consider doing a practice run the day before, to make sure you know exactly how to get there.

Do speak up and present clearly. Ask if they have any questions about your work.

Do use your intuition. Keep an eye on your audience. Make sure they are paying attention. If they look like they are anxious, you might be taking too long—speed it up. If they look confused, pause and ask them if they have any questions.

Do make sure you follow up after your interview. Send a thank you note or email.

143

Top 5 tips for interviewing success
By Sarah Gray, Senior Creative Recruiter, Squarespace, Brooklyn, New York
Elena Anderson, Recruitment & Operations Manager, ustwo, New York
Margaret Morales, Recruiter, Huge, Brooklyn, New York
Danielle Song, Talent Operations Coordinator, Huge, Brooklyn, New York

Recruiters have seen it all. Get inside their heads and understand what they're looking for when sourcing candidates. Four Creative Recruiters share four tips that make the biggest impact when it comes to making a good impression.

Tip 1: Work on your technical skills
Your ability to work through a problem, and design a solution is called technical skills. Although your interviewing experience will be different at every company, these are examples of categories that you and your work may be assessed on.

Execution: Is the design clean? Are the pixels perfect? If we are evaluating from a purely visual perspective, is there a level of refinement to the work?

Systems Design vs. Expressive Design: Have you built a design system from scratch? How often do you work with style guides and component libraries? Do you demonstrate expressive and conceptual design, or is the work restricted by brand guidelines?

Process: How do you talk through your process from concept, design, and delivery phases? What was your individual contribution on any given project? Can you give examples of how you have partnered with other disciplines?

Communication: How do you identify as a designer? What type of design do you want to be doing? How do you articulate and defend your design decisions, both internally and externally?

Tip 2: Be aware of your soft skills: Articulate your passion and make a good first impression
Interviewing success not only about having great craft and a solid portfolio. The way you present yourself, your non-verbal body language, eye contact, managing difficult situations are some of the areas that are called soft skills. Recruiters are paying attention to your soft skills, just as much as your technical skills. Here are a few pointers to make you stand out during your hiring process:

Articulate your passion.

Talk through your experiences. Don't just read from your resume. What were your biggest challenges? Biggest takeaways? Proudest moments?

Speak to your work and your experiences clearly. Avoid rambling sentences. This is your story so make sure you have direction. You may be evaluated on presentation skills and ability to speak to clients.

Be able to talk about why you chose to apply to this specific job/company.

Where do you go for inspiration? Be able to talk about what inspires you.

Do you have side hustles, personal projects, or organizations you are involved with? We want to hear what you are passionate about.

Make a good first impression

Be yourself, and be consistent. The way you conduct yourself in front of the interviewers, the recruiter, and the folks at reception should not be drastically different.

Read the room. Take note of the way that recruiters and interviewers speak with you or talk about the role. This will give you a better idea of what the environment is like at this company.

The way you talk about challenging situations will show how you deal with conflict.

If you're nervous, it's okay to say so!

144

Tip 3: Do your homework
Look at the company's website. Who are their clients? What kind of work do they do? Did they feature any projects? What did you find most interesting about the website?

Do a quick read on what industry publications say about this company (for example: Adweek, Digiday, Agency Spy, Business Insider, Fast Company, award show sites like AWWWARDS, One Show, Cannes).

If you have a list of who will be interviewing you, research their LinkedIn profiles and personal websites, and be ready to ask specific questions about their role or background. These people might become your teammates or manager!

Use LinkedIn to research anyone who currently works or previously worked at that company, and ask to talk about their experience.

Tip 4: Ask the right questions
Interviews are a chance for you to ask recruiters and interviewers questions and assess your fit within the organization. Here are some great questions and common pitfalls.

Tailor your questions to the right person.

Some questions may be more appropriate to ask one person vs. another.

Questions for the recruiter
These are questions better suited for your recruiter, to find out about compensation, salary, and the hiring process, especially in the latter stages of the interview process:

"What are your benefits?"

"What do you pay for this role?"

"What are next steps?"

Questions for the hiring team
These are questions for the interviewers, to find out if the role is the right fit for you:

What types of projects can a designer at my level expect to work on?

What is the relationship between designers and other disciplines (tech, UX, strategy, etc.)?

What are the biggest challenges that someone in this position will be stepping into off the bat?

What does success in the first year look like for this role?

Ask specific questions. Some common generic questions can be asked in more specific manner. Here are common questions that recruiters and interviewers hear all the time, and better way you can ask for information.

Generic: "What is my promotion path?"
Specific: Ask about mentorship and what growth looks like at this company.

Generic: "What is the culture like?"
Specific: You can likely get a sense of a company's culture from their website. Are there other facets to the culture that you are curious about? Is the company affiliated with any volunteer groups or organizations? Do employees engage in team outings or building exercises? Are there affinity groups?

Generic: "What is the day-to-day?"
Specific: Are there specific responsibilities outlined for this role? Projects ready to be taken on? Weekly meetings or creative syncs?

Tip 5: Be courteous
Be courteous and prompt with your communication. Always ask your recruiter for the emails of the interviewers and send them a thank you message! Don't forget to thank a coordinator for setting the interview up as well.

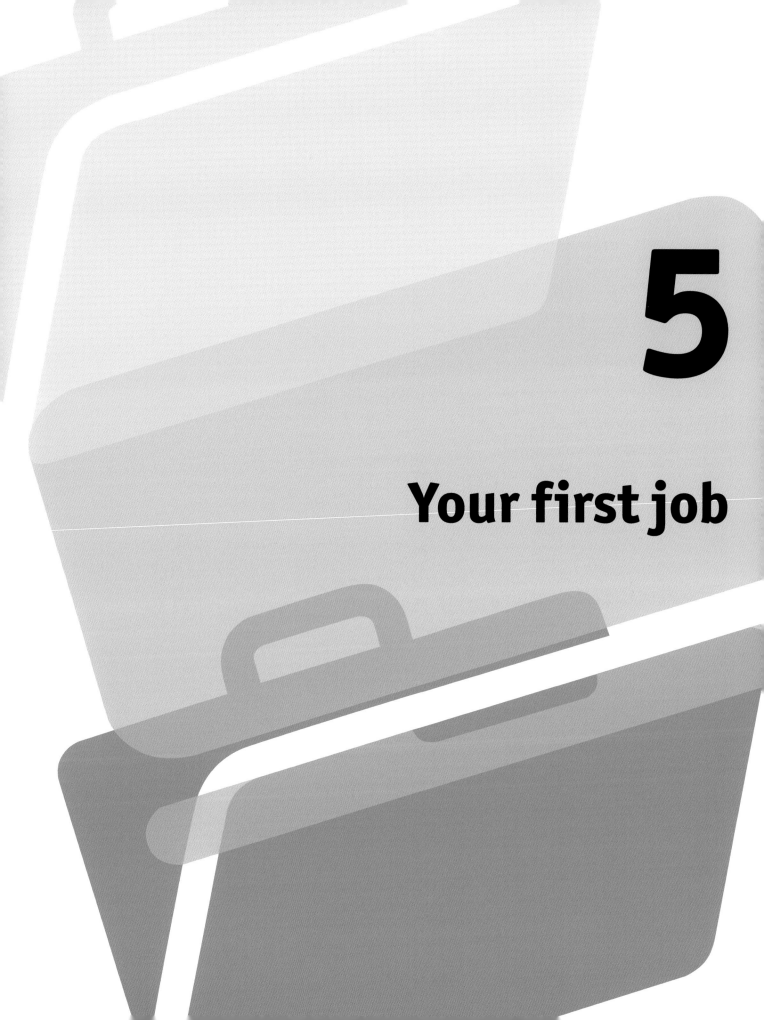

5

Your first job

Your first job might be an internship, a full-time job, or even a first freelance project. This chapter highlights information on important aspects of your first job.

Your first internship

Finding the right internship is an art form. Here are tips and advice from recent grads on the process of finding, applying, and succeeding in internships.

A design internship is one of the most important stepping stones to your professional career. You'll gain real working experience of meeting with teams, collaborating with different disciplines, and potential clients. You'll learn to use your design skills you learned in the classroom and apply it to real challenges.

Getting an internship

Getting a competitive internship is hard work. Timing is everything, and it can be a daunting process. Here is a guideline to get you started on a summer internship, fall internship, and a full-time offer.

Timeline for getting an internship:

Fall of your junior year
> Research companies and agencies
> Network and meet with professionals, alumni, portfolio reviews
> Prepare your portfolio, resume, cover letter
> Find internship job postings

Spring of your junior year
> Apply to internships (January/February)
> Interview (February/March)
> Make your decision, and review your summer internship offers (April)
> Get ready for your internship by securing housing (if needed), collect any necessary paperwork, fill out any HR forms prior to starting your first day

Summer between junior and senior year
> Complete your summer internship (June–August)
> Inquire with your internship employer about a potential extension for a Fall Internship (August)

Fall of your senior year
> Optional: complete a fall internship (September–December)

Spring of your senior year
> Apply for full-time jobs
> Graduate, yay! (May)
> Start your full-time job, fingers crossed (June/July)

148

Tip corner: Advice from recent graduates

My first internship

What was your first internship in the industry?

"My first internship was during the summer after my junior year of college at boutique branding studio in Seattle, Washington, called Mint Design. My portfolio was 90% student work and 10% 'professional' work I made the previous summer when I volunteered with the media team at the Seattle Humane Society. To my surprise, they seemed much more interested in my school projects than the 'professional' work I had." **Anna Rising, Designer & Illustrator, Oslo, Norway (Class of 2015, BFA Graphic Design, University of the Arts in Philadelphia, Pennsylvania)**

"My very first internship was at the in-house studio of my college, The Visual Arts Press, as a design intern. It was during the summer between my sophomore and junior year. I learned so much under the instruction of Gail Anderson and Brian Smith, both amazing designers and mentors. They really set me up for the two other internships that I had afterwards." **Ein Jung, Product Designer, Bunch, New York, New York (Class of 2018, BFA Advertising and Design, School of Visual Arts)**

"My first design internship was at Dunbar Cybersecurity, an IT security company in Hunt Valley, Maryland. I was a summer graphic design intern after I finished my one-year certificate program before starting my first year of MFA." **Hieu Tran, Product Designer, OpenSpace, San Francisco, California (Class of 2016, MFA Graphic Design, Maryland Institute College of Art, Baltimore, Maryland)**

"The summer after my sophomore year at RISD I interned at DWRI Letterpress, a Providence-based letterpress design and production studio, and Design Agency, a local graphic design and branding agency that works exclusively with nonprofit organizations. These were my first professional experiences in the field of design, and I learned a lot through these humble beginnings. These first experiences still have influenced much of my career and perspective on design and collaboration today." **Jason Fujikuni, Art Director, Brand Identity** *The New York Times*, **New York, New York (Class of 2017, BFA Graphic Design, Rhode Island School of Design, Providence, Rhode Island)**

"My first internship was at Thoma Thoma, an advertising agency in Little Rock, Arkansas. I was a summer design intern between my sophomore and junior year. My second internship was with Littlefield, an ad agency in Tulsa, Oklahoma." **Julia Whitley, Graphic Designer, Barkley, Kansas City, Missouri (Class of 2017, BFA Graphic Design, Oklahoma State University, Stillwater, Oklahoma)**

"I consider my apprenticeship with Cyrus Highsmith, founder of Occupant Fonts, my first internship in the type industry. I worked out of Cyrus' garage studio and had lunch with his family in his house. This apprenticeship was very different from what one expects from a usual internship in that I was designing my own typeface the whole time with Cyrus' guidance. I had designed only one unpublished typeface at this point, and this one summer I spent learning from him was the most valuable time career-wise. I learned a ton and met a lot of type designers through him. Now I work with him." **June Shin, Type Designer, Occupant Fonts/Morisawa USA, Providence, Rhode Island (Class of 2017, MFA Graphic Design, Rhode Island School of Design, Providence, Rhode Island)**

149

Tip corner: Advice from recent graduates

"My first internship was as a Graphic Designer at a real estate company in Midtown Manhattan named Highline Residential. It was a joint company that also owned and operated out of a co-working space called Ensemble, which I also did design work for. I started working there in the summer after my Junior year and had no professional experience as designer, let alone in an office setting." **Linnea Taylor, Multimedia Designer, School of Visual Arts, New York, New York (Class of 2016, BFA Design, School of Visual Arts, New York, New York)**

"My first internship was at the School of Visual Arts in-house design team called the Visual Arts Press in Manhattan. I was offered the internship by my interactive design professor junior year." **Masha Vainblat, Senior Digital Designer at Steven Madden, LTD, Long Island City, New York (Class of 2016, BFA Design, School of Visual Arts, New York, New York)**

"My first internship in the industry was at the Visual Arts Press, the design studio for the School of Visual Arts. I was a summer design intern there between my sophomore and junior year of college." **Yejee Pae, Junior Designer, Communal Creative, New York, New York (Class of 2018, BFA Design, School of Visual Arts, New York, New York)**

How I got an internship

How was the internship application and interview process for you?

"I initially found this studio by Googling 'Design Studios in Seattle,' which is where I am from and would spend my summers between school years. When I was in school I made a huge list of studios that I liked in different cities that I wanted to live in, and when it came time to applying to internships I would go through the list and email all of them. A lot of larger studios and agencies had application deadlines for summer internships in March, so the earlier you start this process the better. I quickly found that even if a studio doesn't have a listing about an open job, it never hurts to send an email and apply anyways! That's how I landed the gig at Mint Design." **Anna Rising, Designer & Illustrator, Oslo, Norway (Class of 2015, BFA Graphic Design, University of the Arts in Philadelphia, Pennsylvania)**

"I was lucky to have experienced a wide range of workplaces within the industry throughout my four years in college. From small design studios to global agencies, I learned about the pros and cons of the various settings a designer could work in. I think it's important to get a taste of different studios/agencies while you're in school. It's the only way to learn what suits you best." **Ein Jung, Product Designer, Bunch, New York, New York (Class of 2018, BFA Advertising and Design, School of Visual Arts, New York, New York)**

"From what I have seen so far, the application and interview process for design internships varies a lot from corporate companies to design studios/agencies to startups. For the most part, it is really is a number game, so definitely apply to as many places as you can. Usually, I start 2–3 months in advance, and it really helps if you know someone who is already working at the place you are interested in applying because then they can pass your name along. There are so many job boards on the internet where you can look for internships (examples: Design Observer, Dribble, Behance, SPD, etc.). But my favorite thing to do is going through a list of design studios/agencies from studio-index.co, find cool places with amazing work, look at their career pages, and then apply if there is an open position.

Once you start hearing back from places, it's time to talk. I find it challenging with those long Google Hangout calls because you are talking to a screen—so a helpful tip is to make sure you are in a quiet room with no distractions, and please have good WiFi. There might be time when you think a particular internship isn't as good as some other ones, but I would still highly encourage you to take on the conversation because (1) you will never know the kind of connections you will make with the recruiters/designers that you talk to and (2) you get better at talking about yourself and your work.

Here are a few things I learned.

One: If a place gives off bad vibes or does not want to pay you: do not take it. It is okay to turn places down, you just have to be respectful about it.

Two: If a place takes too long to get back to you, it is okay to follow up. Don't sit around and wait.

Three, once you accept an offer to a place, be mindful and let the other places you are talking to know." **Hieu Tran, Product Designer, OpenSpace, San Francisco, California (Class of 2016, MFA Graphic Design, Maryland Institute College of Art, Baltimore, Maryland)**

"I typically began researching studios and companies I was interested in for a summer internship around January. I was fortunate to have had a work study job at the career center on campus, and part of my daily responsibilities was talking to employers and posting job and internship opportunities on our career portal. I would submit numerous applications and send cold-call emails to studios and agencies that I liked, inquiring if they would take me as an intern. Many of my professors were generous to help provide some connections as well; the first internships I had were with the studios my professors worked at. The internship and job applying process can take a lot out of you, and I always felt that it was important to remind myself that it's a learning experience, and that every rejection draws you closer to the right opportunity. With uncertainty there is both great excitement and opportunity." **Jason Fujikuni, Art Director, Brand Identity *The New York Times*, New York, New York (Class of 2017, BFA Graphic Design, Rhode Island School of Design, Providence, Rhode Island)**

"The biggest lessons I learned from my internships were in the interview process. Writing a cover letter, having a well designed resume, having a PDF portfolio, all of those things are so important, so it's nice having a practice run with an internship. Also, being able to interview and get a glimpse of the common questions asked by companies definitely helps you prepare for future interviews. You also learn a lot about rejection. I was rejected or ignored a lot during my internship search and that prepared me to have thick skin when it came to job hunting. You can't get disheartened by rejection or radio silence from companies, all you can do is keep applying and keep trying until you find the right fit. One of the biggest lessons I learned from the actual internship was that even if it isn't everything you wanted it to be, you have still gained valuable experience and have a better idea of the kind of place you want to work." **Julia Whitley, Graphic Designer, Barkley, Kansas City, Missouri (Class of 2017, BFA Graphic Design, Oklahoma State University, Stillwater, Oklahoma)**

151

Tip corner: Advice from recent graduates

"There was no application or interview, as Cyrus Highsmith was my teacher at RISD and he knew me well. I simply had to express my interest in type design and ask if he knew of any internship opportunities. He didn't, but instead, he offered me something better." **June Shin, Type Designer, Occupant Fonts/Morisawa USA, Providence, Rhode Island (Class of 2017, MFA Graphic Design, Rhode Island School of Design, Providence, Rhode Island)**

"I was able to get my first internship through a friend of mine, who at the time was the Creative Director for Highline Residential. He mentioned how his current intern was leaving towards the end of the summer, and I saw the opportunity to ask if he would be interested in bringing me on as her replacement. I brought my printed portfolio to the interview, which he and his current intern browsed and inquired about, and then they showed me different projects they were working on or had completed recently. Thankfully, the interview was very casual, so I felt comfortable making jokes and being myself. A big part of hiring can be seeing if you and your team can work with the candidate and enjoy your time together, so try and relax as much as you can and see where the conversation can take you.

It was definitely beneficial in familiarizing myself with an office setting and interacting with people from various departments. I learned that I preferred working in a smaller company such as Highline because you're able to get to know people at all ranks of the company and as you get more familiar, your confidence grows in your ability to make decisions, take control of situations, and bring ideas to the table that will benefit everyone involved.

I'm thankful, and quite lucky, to be able to make a connection that gave me foot in the door, but that was something my teachers and the chair of the program at SVA really pushed, and I continue to follow and give that same advice to every young designer needing insight. Connections are a huge part of the industry—whether it's fellow artists, teachers, or friends—and you'd be surprised how many opportunities arise. When you work hard, people around you take notice and want to help you continue to succeed." **Linnea Taylor, Multimedia Designer, School of Visual Arts, New York, New York (Class of 2016, BFA Design, School of Visual Arts, New York, New York)**

"I had been interning every summer since the beginning of my college career. Luckily, I had the opportunity to work for VAP after my interactive design professor offered me a position. I loved that I was able to give back to the SVA community from within the establishment by helping with design tasks such as redesigning parts of the SVA.edu website. Hard work goes a long way, and all though this opportunity presented itself, I was never afraid to take advantage of the resources available to me, such as the hard working and talented faculty at SVA. Multiple internship and job opportunities simply came from the classroom setting and relationships with my professors." **Masha Vainblat, Senior Digital Designer at Steven Madden, LTD, Long Island City, New York (Class of 2016, BFA Design, School of Visual Arts, New York, New York)**

"I started doing research for potential internships during winter break. I just explored and discovered what my options were. I really started to apply to places in April/May after I had a pdf of my portfolio or a link to my website with all my most recent work available to show. Honestly speaking, all the internships I landed in college were through my college professors who referred me. It is incredibly important to have a relationship with your instructors at SVA because they have a network of people they know, and their reference for you will be much more effective than sending off your resume and portfolio to 50 studios. My final piece of advice is that your portfolio work will get you maybe 40% of the way to a job. The other 60% is really how you present yourself and talk about your projects, your attitude, and how your personality will fit into the workplace. In every place that I interview, I think about what I have to offer to them, but mostly what I can learn by working in that environment." **Yejee Pae, Junior Designer, Communal Creative, New York, New York (Class of 2018, BFA Design, School of Visual Arts, New York, New York)**

How did you make the most of your internship?

"As cliché as is sounds, don't be afraid to ask questions. Working in a professional environment is heaps different than school, and since internships are usually fairly short, the best way to really get a grasp on what the professional world is like is to dive right in. Also, make connections! Take advantage of building relationships with other designers and people you admire. Surrounding yourself with great designers and people you admire is a really great form of motivation." **Anna Rising, Designer & Illustrator, Oslo, Norway (Class of 2015, BFA Graphic Design, University of the Arts in Philadelphia, Pennsylvania)**

What is your biggest advice to getting the most out of your internship experience?

"Be hyper-aware of everything that goes on. Even if it's not related to what you major in, it's always good to pick up new knowledge about the inner workings of the workplace. Be eager to work on small things and do it gratefully." **Ein Jung, Product Designer, Bunch, New York, New York (Class of 2018, BFA Advertising and Design, School of Visual Arts, New York, New York)**

"Be honest to whoever you are reporting to about what you are hoping to learn. It is not always easy to speak up when you feel small being an intern—but if you work with the right people, they will listen and support you." **Hieu Tran, Product Designer, OpenSpace, San Francisco, California (Class of 2016, MFA Graphic Design, Maryland Institute College of Art, Baltimore, Maryland)**

"Speak up and be a sponge. I am fortunate to have had great internship experiences in the arc of my career at RISD, but I definitely wish I had spent more time connecting with my coworkers and the people around me, and less time trying to prove myself or worrying about being fired. An internship experience should be beneficial for both you and the employer; it is a learning experience and opportunity for you to figure out where your interests are in design and to acquire professional experience. No one expects you to know everything; you are there to learn, contribute and offer new ideas. Make the most of the experience and have fun! Be sure to take time to explore the city you are in also, your surroundings are as much of the internship experience as the studio/company you are interning at." **Jason Fujikuni, Art Director, Brand Identity *The New York Times*, New York, New York (Class of 2017, BFA Graphic Design, Rhode Island School of Design, Providence, Rhode Island)**

"The biggest advice I could give to someone who wants to get the most out of their internship is to not be afraid to ask for help or ask questions. I thought that if I asked for help they would think I was incompetent or not good enough, but that is not the case. You are there to learn, and the people you are working for know what it takes to get a job after college so utilize them. Especially when it comes to your portfolio. Don't be afraid to ask them to look at your portfolio and critique it, and thank them a lot when they do because they probably have given you valuable insight you would not have got anywhere else. I would also encourage them to get to know their fellow interns, if there are others. I have seen interns get super competitive with each other because they thought if they tried to be better than everyone else they would get the job, but that will usually backfire. Companies want to hire team players who work well with others. In my second internship I met a girl who was interning with the account side and now she is one of my best friends." **Julia Whitley, Graphic Designer, Barkley, Kansas City, Missouri (Class of 2017, BFA Graphic Design, Oklahoma State University, Stillwater, Oklahoma)**

153

Tip corner: Advice from recent graduates

"Don't wait for someone to give you a task. Take initiatives and go above and beyond. On the other hand, if you find yourself in an internship that has nothing to offer you, have the courage to pack up and leave. Your time is better spent elsewhere where your skills are valued and you have an opportunity to grow." **June Shin, Type Designer, Occupant Fonts/Morisawa USA, Providence, Rhode Island (Class of 2017, MFA Graphic Design, Rhode Island School of Design, Providence, Rhode Island)**

"The best advice is to get out there and get your foot in the door. It doesn't need to be your dream job or at the company you want to ultimately end up at—experience is experience. Some internships may be great, some may be bad, but working in different environments helps you understand what atmosphere you create best in, what types of people you get along with, and what kind of position or industry you find most satisfying." **Linnea Taylor, Multimedia Designer, School of Visual Arts, New York, New York (Class of 2016, BFA Design, School of Visual Arts, New York, New York)**

"Work hard and try to learn as much as you can. Get to know as many people as you can to truly immerse yourself in the experience." **Masha Vainblat, Senior Digital Designer at Steven Madden, LTD, Long Island City, New York (Class of 2016, BFA Design, School of Visual Arts, New York, New York)**

"Throughout my work experience, it's less about proving yourself as a designer, and more about your openness to communicate, being transparent and showing an eagerness to learn, grow, and collaborate with your coworkers throughout the process. I don't look for work that is just going to look glittery on my resume. I look for places where I can flourish, not only as a designer but also as a human being." **Yejee Pae, Junior Designer, Communal Creative, New York, New York (Class of 2018, BFA Design, School of Visual Arts, New York, New York)**

154

Your first full-time job

You received your official full-time job offer, signed it, and you're about to start on Monday. Congratulations! This career advice will help you succeed in your first "real world" job to jumpstart your professional design life.

Create your 30-60-90 plan

Your first 90 days at the company are often considered an extension of your interview process. During this initial period, your team and manager are will be getting to know you and how you work, and likewise, as you should use this time to understand the breadth of work, company culture and expectations to ensure that this job was the right decision for you.

Once you've completed orientation and spent a couple of weeks familiarizing yourself with the company, work, and the team, consider speaking to your manager to create your own 30-60-90-day plan. This is a list of short-term, attainable goals and tasks you can do during your first, second, and third month on the job.

Keep learning

Stay inspired, passionate, and relevant with professional development. Once you've settled into your new job, look for ways to develop yourself professionally. For example, your company may offer internal training sessions or a mentoring program. Or may be interested in taking continuing education classes at a nearby university or education center like General Assembly, or enrolling in online courses through Skillshare, Lynda. com, CodeCademy, or Coursera.

Other professional development opportunities are attending conferences, workshops, and supplementing your on-the-job training with career development books, podcasts, and videos.

Build your professional network

A strong professional network will not only help you land your first job, but it will support your career down the line, when you find yourself needing advice from a mentor or connecting to the next step (should you find yourself unemployed or looking for a new job).

5 ways to build a strong network

1. Check out your for university's alumni events and connect with your former classmates and professors.
2. Join LinkedIn groups, and find other relevant professional associations online.
3. Find groups on MeetUp and EventBrite events on topics that interest you.
4. Attend conferences, workshops, and trade shows.
5. Use social networks (LinkedIn, Facebook, Instagram, Twitter) to connect to different people in the design industry.

Track your accomplishments

With so much to do at your new job, it's easy to lose track of your work and accomplishments. Consider keeping a running list of your wins in Google Drive, Evernote, or a notebook tucked away in your desk. This will allow you to keep track of everything you've accomplished prepared for your annual review, or when you're exploring new opportunities.

155

Save your work

This one might seem obvious, but keep a copy of all your work for your portfolio. Be sure you don't upload any sensitive client work to your public portfolio without getting permission from your manager. Upload, celebrate, and promote your work once the project is live and you have permission to post it online.

Stay inspired

There is nothing more important to a company than hiring the best and the brightest people, who are already curious, active, and interested in the design and advertising industry. You can't be inspiring, if you are not inspired. Here is a list of publications, podcasts, videos, and events to keep you inspired:

The bare-bones minimum reading are industry sites like AdAge, AdWeek, Digiday, and Agency Spy, as well as general-interest publications like *Forbes*, *Fast Company*, *Tech Crunch*, and *The New York Times*.

Podcasts like Debbie Millman's "Design Matters" and "Adventures in Design," as well as general-interest podcasts like NPR "Radio Lab," and TED Talks.

Classic design and advertising books are David Ogilvy *On Advertising*, Tim Brown *Change by Design*, and David Kelley *Creative Confidence*, and the classic Dale Carnegie *How to Influence People*.

Next, there are inspiring documentaries on design, like "Helvetica," "Eames," Massimo Vignelli's "Design is One," Milton Glaser's "To Inform and Delight," "Beautiful Losers," and the "Abstract" documentary series on Netflix.

Finally attending events, talks, conferences, workshops and seminars through AIGA, TDC, ADC, SPD, AWNY, NYC UXPA, and even museums at the MoMA are another source of inspiration.

Workplace politics 101

This is tough to summarize, but an important topic you won't learn in the classroom. There are whole books dedicated to this important topic that might be worth referencing to help you gain a deeper understanding of workplace politics.

Workplace politics is about teamwork, transparency, ethics, knowing the value of keeping your mouth shut sometimes, looking out for people working outside the team, knowing when to put things in writing, and when to speak privately.

Keep hustlin'

Whether it's freelancing on the side, running a personal online boutique selling prints of your photography, serving your community, or teaching—the best professional designers find time to pursue their passion outside of their full-time work. A side hustle balance is a great way to stay inspired, learn new skills, meet new people, and earn additional income.

Ask the professionals: My side hustle

Finding a balance between building a career and enjoying side projects

Do you have a side project? What's your secret to balancing a side project with your day job?

"I am currently renovating and reviving an historic 1938 roadside motel and tavern in the Catskills called the Red Rose. It's a passion project my husband and I took on two years ago. We wanted to give back to the community we've spent weekends traveling to and relaxing in over the years.

The secret to balancing, is to work with people you love and trust and that compliment the skills and abilities you have, in both your day job and your side projects. Make these efforts worth your time and something you enjoy. I've learned to be patient and understand that things worth doing are worth doing well. For us It'll be an ongoing effort as we get the business up and running. It won't be done in a short time frame or all at once. Build on the small successes.

In general, try to do something bold and exciting that you have no business doing. Take risks and have fun along the way. It's super hard and doesn't always turn out as you thought it might, but it makes you a much more interesting person in the end for having tried." **Kris Kiger, Executive Vice President, Executive Creative Director, Design, R/GA, New York, New York**

"I love writing children's books in my free time. But that free time is extremely sporadic, and hasn't given me the chance to actually pitch them to publishers.

My other side project is my kids. My secret to balancing them into my day job is simply to not work weekends. With very very rare exceptions, I give them all my attention when I'm with them, which means they rejuvenate me for my work and my work rejuvenates me to be with them." **Emily Wengert, Group Vice President, User Experience, Huge, Brooklyn, New York**

"I've always had stuff going on in the background; books, freelance projects, teaching. I thrive on juggling lots of projects, for better or worse. You have to try to compartmentalize things and not let your worlds collide too much if you take on outside work. I have no secret to share—it's about wanting to stay fresh challenged, and it doesn't hurt to have a little extra money coming in." **Gail Anderson, Chair, BFA Design and BFA Advertising, Creative Director, Visual Arts Press, School of Visual Arts, New York, New York**

"I have side projects and ideas, always. I reserve that for one day of the weekend. That's the beauty and horror of being a designer. Our curiosity doesn't stop!" **Ida Woldemichael, Associate Creative Director, Wide Eye, Washington D.C.**

"Yes, always. I'm always producing some side projects for fun, to test new things, to prove myself, to get out of the comfort zone. I try to be as methodical at work as when I'm having fun with my side projects. There has to be a commitment, otherwise nothing happens. Now, for example, I am developing an oil paintings project, and at the same time, I am helping to develop the expansion of my startup, an app with almost 200M users." **Fred Saldanha, Global Chief Creative Officer, VMLY&R, New York, New York**

"I love making books. There's something about creating physical objects that you can hold in your hand that can't be beat by digital. I also want to have artifacts of my work that will last forever in the real world and not sit digitally on a hard drive somewhere." **Ryan Scott Tandy, Product Design Manager, Instagram, San Francisco, California**

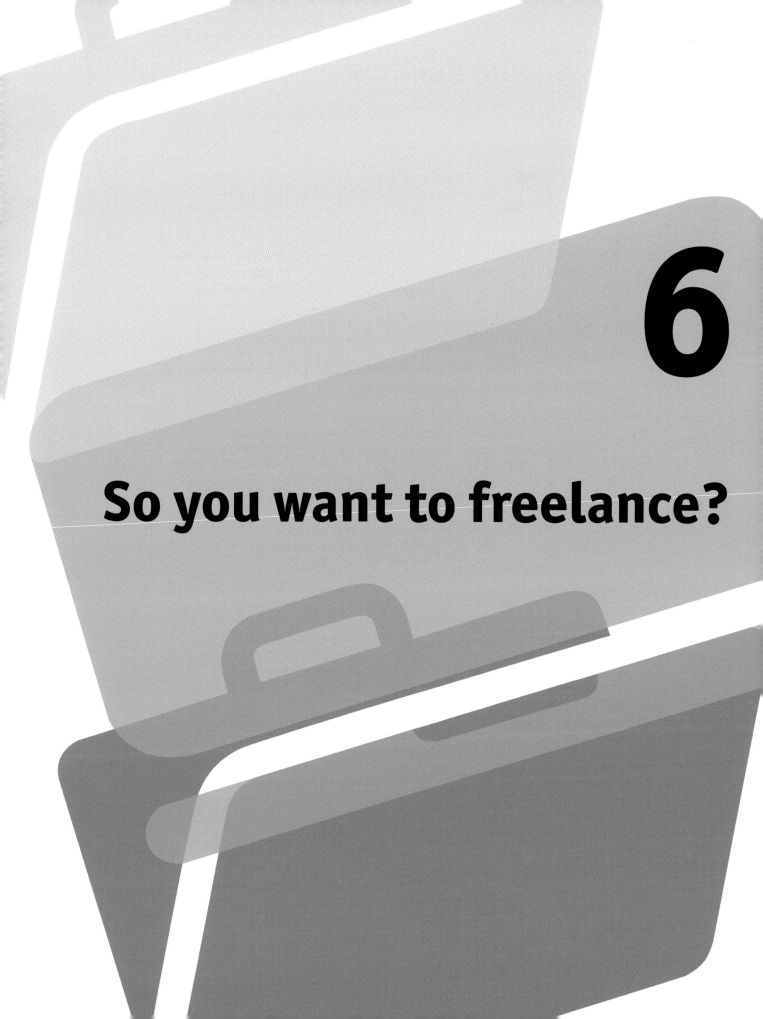

6

So you want to freelance?

Freelance can be exciting and scary at the same time. You can ease your way into freelance by taking on a few freelance projects while you still have a full-time job. While freelance allows you the flexibility to have more personal time off, work in new environments and meet new people on a regular basis, it also requires a demanding self-promotion effort and financial management.

This chapter will cover the pros and cons of freelancing, advice on money, taxes, self-promotion, and pricing. Professional freelance designers will provide their insight and experience so you can make the right decision if freelancing is right for you.

The pros and cons of freelancing

Freelancing can be empowering, especially if you're feeling stuck or burnt out from your full-time job. However, freelancing comes with important considerations. Are you prepared financially and mentally prepared to be on your own?

Explore this table to find out.

Pros

Can be freeing and relaxing

More personal time off

Exposure to different offices and work environments

Meet new people

Work with different teams

Flexibility in assignments and clients

Cons

You're not a part of the company culture, and are often excluded from company events

No health/dental/vision insurance, you'll need to pay for your own insurance

Can be challenging to transition back to full-time

Instability in consistent work

No pay raises (unless you jump around a lot)

No paid time off (federal holidays, vacation, sick days are all unpaid)

Significant amount of time needs to be spent networking and making connections to line up your next gig

Need to have at least six months of savings

Inconsistent paychecks

High administrative overhead (writing invoices, keeping track of invoices, doing taxes, keeping track of all expenses)

Minimal mentorship or coaching at the company

Ask the professionals: My experience as a freelance designer

The pros and cons of going freelance

What do you like and dislike about your experience as a freelancer?

"My favorite thing about freelancing is that I feel like the clients I work for respect me more as a professional than if I was working as a full-time employee. The ability to negotiate for oneself is vital to being a good freelancer. It has made me better at marketing my own schools and has taught me how to tell the story of my career in a more cohesive way. It has made me more confident in the quality of the work I do because during interviews I have had to look critically back at the work and describe it in a way that I never would have done as an employee. My least favorite thing is that usually as a motion design freelancer I am brought in towards the end of a project to complete a very specific task. I like to think more broadly about projects and especially on pitches or during specific crunch times I am usually tasked with taking an already set design and animate it. This usually means that I don't get to think about an experience holistically and I am just trying to get a job done. Another thing I dislike about freelancing is that it is much harder to integrate into an office environment when you know there is an end date." **Sam Stringer-Hye, Senior Designer, Publicis Sapient, Brooklyn, New York**

"My favorite part about being a freelancer, when things are good, is this feeling of almost complete control of my working life. I feel like I have options for everything I do. I might have a selection of projects to choose from and if I end up choosing one that isn't what I was expecting, I can end it and find another one—though I make sure to work with the client to do it in a way that is respectful and doesn't leave them in a bad spot.

I can also choose not to work. This comes at the sacrifice of money, but I have that choice. If I want to take a vacation or plan a day or two off, I just do it. I don't have to clear it with any sort of manager or make sure I'm keeping it under a set amount of days. I own that time and can choose whether I want it for myself or if I want to spend it working.

My least favorite part comes when things are bad. After a couple of weeks without work (unplanned), it starts to take a toll mentally. The unplanned days are nice at first, I can check out museums, restaurants, and places that are too crowded on weekends for me to visit. Then I start to think that maybe the economy is turning around and I shouldn't be spending money at these places. . . and maybe I should start looking at full-time positions for the sake of stability.

Then there are thoughts of self-doubt. I start thinking that maybe I'm not that great of a designer and that I've just been extremely lucky, or my work is starting to become dated and stale. Maybe I should just take that banner production job because that's what I really should be doing.

But the one thing I've learned over the past 4+ years (as well as talking to other freelancers) is that everything comes in waves. I can go three weeks without work, then one day I'll wake up to multiple job inquiries and things are good again.

Fortunately things have been good way more than they have been bad. So those episodes of mild depression and self-doubt are far and few between (and slightly exaggerated)." **Michael Mitzman, Freelance Designer & Art Director, Brooklyn, New York**

"Working as a freelancer you have to be able to adapt to your environment. As long as you set expectations you can avoid any mismatching bookings or working on projects that may be out of your depth. In the beginning of your career, you might not be on the most interesting projects but use this as a moment to grow and learn a new skill set. I always try to look for something positive I can take away from any experience. If I realize that a specific studio or client is not a good fit for me, there is no need work with them in the future. One of the benefits of being self-employed is to be able to choose who and what you work on and with. I found out, the hard way, that I do not enjoy working on show packages for broadcast. Specifically, making tool kits in AfterEffects. I remember one instance I stayed at a studio until 1am rushing to deliver a tool kit and thought to myself, 'This is definitely not for me.' Again, I used this moment to understand my strengths and weaknesses and grew from there." **Tyler Wergin, Freelance Designer and Animator, New York, New York**

"I have been freelancing for less than 2 years and have worked mostly in the digital branding and product design space. I have worked with start-ups at 15 person agencies like Free Association to much larger clients at high profile shops like Huge.

My favorite part about freelancing is the variety—both in work and the environments. I tend to have engagements that range anywhere from 6 weeks to 3 months and have been very fortunate enough to have had the offer of extending my contract at most places. The down side of freelancing is the unknown periods where there's an absence of work. During that time I tend to update my portfolio with my latest projects and teach myself new skills. As a freelancer it's important to keep yourself marketable by following the latest design news and staying up to date of the latest software and tools.

There's always something to learn and freelancing has given me the challenge of keeping my skills sharp as well as learning a sense of how to position myself as a independent and highly capable designer. I find that being smart and collaborative goes a long way. Being able to do great work is important, but being friendly and easygoing during high-stress situations (often the case when you are called in) will take you far and consistently booked." **Amanda R. George, Senior Design Lead, Huge, Brooklyn, New York**

"Freelancing is not stable financially. You have to be smart with saving money. Some people find that difficult, but you will master that aspect experience.

Second and maybe more important than money, is taking vacation, and time to do 'nothing.' Vacations are so important, and as an independent contractor, you will always find yourself in situations where you have free time, and you think, 'I have time to go on vacation, should I go somewhere?' but you get an offer for a new project, and you start to shifting and moving your vacation for the next month and so on. . . and then you hardy you take any vacations because you are always chasing new clients and projects. It gets difficult to decide if you should take time to vacation, when it has a financial impact on your income. But, you need to do it, otherwise we will burn out. As designers and artists, we depend not only from our skill set, but we also need to discover the world, learn new things and live new experiences in order to came up with ideas. We need to have knowledge about the world we are working for, we need to be universal—and you can not become universal by watching YouTube and creating beautiful Pinterest boards. My advice is to book your tickets 6 months ahead, and you will have no excuse to not do travel. Please take vacation!" **Cristian Vargas, Designer and Associate Creative Director, Brooklyn, New York**

"As to everything else, there are up and downsides to freelancing. Some people like freelancing because it gives them flexibility, some prefer to be full-time for the steady paychecks and being part of a larger team. There is no right or wrong answer, it really just depends on your personality and your goals in life.

For me, the best part about freelancing is the people you meet along the way. I have met many interesting people during my freelance career, some of which are also my best friends today. As fellow freelancers, it is easy and natural to connect with one another. I have a freelancer friend who is also a travel photographer; another is a touring musician. I am still amazed how they manage their work arrangements and do all of that part time.

I am able to be selective with the projects that I take on. I am not confined to one specific type of projects and clients. You could be working on a branding project one day, and digital product work the next. The variety is an important aspect of freelancing that is really appealing to me.

Being a freelancer is like being an entrepreneur; your product is your craft and service. You are essentially a one-man business. With that come responsibilities and challenges that designers usually do not encounter in staff positions. Those being financial planning for your business, project management, dealing with subcontractors, negotiating contracts. Sometimes it's about being comfortable to step outside of your role as designers to take the project over the finish line. I certainly have had fair share of being a producer for photo shoots, or doubling up as product manager for site developments. It is the nature of the beast, I've come to accept that over the year. I do not think it is a bad thing; if anything I've grown and learned to be more adaptive.

The biggest downside to me is that oftentimes the uncertainties around the timeline of projects. It is hard enough to line up the contracts so you can transition from one gig to another without the clients pushing back on the timeline or canceling last minute. It is hard to plan my personal life around the assignments because I don't want to miss out on the work. In advertising, for example, this happens quite often because the projects get put on hold or pushed back after you got booked for the gig. Flaky recruiters can also be a big issue, there are some who only pop up when they need someone to fill a spot the next day or so, which is crazy since most people cannot just drop their current project and jump on those types of assignment.

Another downside of freelancing is that majority of the time, you are working with limited information or support. There are times when I were asked to work with a team on projects that I absolutely have no context or background. As a designer, information is crucial to making the right judgments on the solutions that you are providing. When you work on a deliverable for a client, you need to know what goals they are trying to achieve, and how did the ask came along in the first place, in order to address the problems effectively. Without proper information, you would always be one step behind everyone else, and that would inevitably affect your outputs. That comes from poor management, this happened to me, and to many other freelancers that I have talked to over the years. It is rather unfortunate that your work is not always judged in its entirety, and it is definitely a turnoff for a lot of freelancers. That said, not all projects and studios are disorganized." **Long Vu, Art Director & Designer, Brooklyn, New York, Brooklyn, New York**

How did you make the transition into freelancing?

"I ultimately made a leap of faith into freelancing. I was at a full-time job as an Art Director at a company and was succumbing to burn out due to a lot of layoffs and a toxic work environment. I had a colleague/mentor who agreed that we needed to get out together. Luckily he is much more extroverted than I am and was better at getting clients for social media marketing design work. He handled working with the clients and some copywriting while I handled design and animation work. It was a good situation and was a great way to have a safety net for the first months of work. Over time I developed my own clients and had a few repeat projects. It was great learning experience that I just threw myself into." **Sam Stringer-Hye, Senior Designer, Publicis Sapient, Brooklyn, New York**

"There was never a moment in which I thought freelancing would be the right for me. I had been working at an agency for 3 years and how I was growing as a designer just wasn't lining up with how the agency was evolving and I knew I needed a change.

One day I was briefed in on a project that I really did not want to do and came back the following morning and put in my 2 weeks. I didn't have much of a plan in place, but I figured I could freelance until I found a full-time job that felt right to me.

However, I was expecting that there would immediately be work for me. It took about a month for me to get my name and book out there and for a project to actually lineup. I slowly started getting more and more freelance offers for work that I was enjoying and I just stopped considering full-time work." **Michael Mitzman, Freelance Designer & Art Director, Brooklyn, New York**

"My leap into freelance was a sink or swim moment. Less than a week after graduating college, I moved to New York with big dreams, a few friends, and no money. I didn't have a job or interview lined up, but I was very passionate and determined to make it work. I started with emailing other artists seeking advice and to my surprise a lot of people were willing to help me land my first job. Though it is a competitive market, the freelance community is relatively small and helping one another is key to success. Another thing that I think helped me was positioning. Instead of emailing producers my reel and saying that I'm a recent grad looking for work, etc. I played the part of already being in the industry and that I was available for freelance. My only option was to make freelancing work. I had no other life raft." **Tyler Wergin, Freelance Designer and Animator, New York, New York**

"I worked for companies for about 5 years and then I moved into an independent career. I always knew that I will be independent, because I don't like routines and environments affect me in a positive and negative way. For example, I like having 2 desks, I usually have a desk for crafts and the other desk for my computer and digital/electronic devices. Oftentimes, in office spaces you do not have the opportunity to have this setup. I work a lot on paper, then I scan something, then I re-draw on the computer, then I print it, then I redraw on that printed paper and so on. . . so more experimental/flexible spaces are better for me and for my personality. Sometimes I just don't have the energy to work on something and all what I want to do is just go for a ride and read something or take photos. The funny thing is that sometimes you work way more hours as an independent freelancer, than an employee, but for me it is more rewarding. So my transition was easy because I knew what I need to be happy and comfortable to create ideas, but not that easy at the beginning trying to chase projects and clients. But everything is about time, so if you are passionate and focused on what you want, you will get it sooner or later." **Cristian Vargas, Designer and Associate Creative Director, Brooklyn, New York**

"I spent the first 2.5 years of my career working as an art director for various record labels, the work is very creative, which is why I loved it in the first place. The medium and the process in that field is very different in comparison to other creative fields; while I absolutely loved what I was doing, music is a very niche field with not a lot of room to grow. Being with the same company for a period of time, I was comfortable with the environment, the people, and the pace of work. I was starting to feel like I hit a wall and stopped growing. There was a freelance opportunity that came along, so I decided to take my chance and start freelancing. During the first year, I freelanced for a startup, a few ad agencies. They are all very different projects, cultures, and timeline; as a creative, the challenge of working with new clients and new projects seemed appealing to me. I stepped out of my comfort zone, it was intimidating at first, but I realized it was great for my personal growth. I was able to learn their processes and improve my design chops in short period of time. I learned to enjoy the unpredictability that comes with freelancing; that is when I know that it was a right choice." **Long Vu, Art Director & Designer, Brooklyn, New York**

What advice would you give to young designers wanting to work for themselves?

"Showing up and being available is half the job. You can only be so talented if you never show up. I think that most clients would prefer a reliable and friendly freelancer than one who is talented but can't be reached. Be concise and clear in your communication with clients. This will save a lot of headaches. Also,

remember that your ultimate goal is to help the client achieve their goals, not to boost your own ego." **Sam Stringer-Hye, Senior Designer, Publicis Sapient, Brooklyn, New York**

"I have two pieces of advice:

1. Work full-time for an agency for a couple of years. There are a lot of things regarding process and business that is unique to design and advertising that you should know and the best way to do that is to be part of it.

This also gives you an opportunity to have mentors and learn from more senior designers. Having people that you see everyday that you can show and talk design with is something that will really help you get better as a designer. Then when you are ready to go freelance, you will also hopefully have a web of connections as people tend to move around a lot.

2. Be reliable and responsive.
I honestly think this alone has gotten me a lot of repeat business.

This sounds obvious, but I have had a large number of hiring managers and creative directors be overly grateful for me hitting deadlines, responding to emails in a reasonable time, and just being easy to work with.

It wasn't until I actually had to hire freelancers of my own that I realized why they were so grateful. I've only had to bring on a few freelancers, but I have had multiple just completely ghost me mid-project, only send me half of the agreed deliverables, or text me the night before a deadline saying that they need more time, all of which completely messed up my work and potentially any repeat business. I then talked to other designers in similar situations as me who have had the same issues. So for whatever reason, this is a common problem in the business (and why I now do all I can to avoid managing people).

You can be an amazing designer, but if you can't hit a deadline or respond to an email, people aren't going to trust you enough to hire you. This is the same for a full-time position as well. Coworkers will remember your attitude and responsiveness, especially once you leave to go freelance and they're elsewhere and need to bring someone in." **Michael Mitzman, Freelance Designer & Art Director, Brooklyn, New York**

"Some advice I can give recent graduates is to stay hungry and passionate about your craft. Understand that you will make mistakes in the beginning, but learn from your mistakes. Have clear goals as to what you want to do and stick to them. Be kind. If you do decide to become self-employed, realize that the industry is smaller than you think and the friendlier you are to people the more jobs you will get. Sometimes it's not always about skill set. If you can work well within a team environment, studios will hire you, and people will want to work with you." **Tyler Wergin, Freelance Designer and Animator, New York, New York**

"I had a few years of full-time experience at R/GA before transitioning to freelance. I actually freelanced right out of school before I landed there, and it was not the best experience. Fresh out of school, my design and presentation skills were not strong and I struggled without a foundation to build off of. Once I attained a full-time Associate Designer role at R/GA that all changed. I was part of the junior talent pool program there that exposed me to different departments within the agency as well as several different accounts. While there, I was able to attain the mentorship, skills, and confidence I needed to get me to where I am today.

While I know some people who have been successful freelancing right out of school, I recommend gaining some consistency in a full-time role before making the switch. It makes the transition much smoother."
Amanda R. George, Senior Design Lead, Huge, Brooklyn, New York

"I think the market seems saturated, but there is always room for new people with new ideas and a different perspective. Companies are looking for people who can change/brake paradigms and challenge the industry. Consider your business card (don't just have a typical business card, be thoughtful about it) and your website (make it more than just a grid with beautiful thumbnails). Plan how you present your work in front of your clients or companies, it's always important to have the unexpected factor. If you can go to a meeting to show your work, it has to be exceptional and memorable. Companies are tired to see the same, so start to define your own identity and the tools you going to use to promote yourself, remember there are thousands like you, so what's makes you different than the rest? Use that as a starting point." **Cristian Vargas, Designer and Associate Creative Director, Brooklyn, New York**

"Some of the general and professional advices I always give to new freelancers are around work ethics and maintaining a work-life balance as they are generally more true across the board:

Learn how to manage your workload to maintain a healthy lifestyle. I have had periods when 3 projects came in at the same time; as a freelancer, I wanted to make sure I can work whenever I can, so I took them all on. Even though I delivered all 3 projects on time, I ended up working nonstop, 12–18 hours a day, for 2–3 weeks straight, even weekends. It was taxing as you can imagine. I think it would be worth it if you were working on something you really love; but not over a long period of time. First, that is not sustainable, and second, the quality of work suffers when you are spread too thin. Only take on projects if you are absolutely sure you have the bandwidth to deliver.

Choose project over money. This is especially important for young designers. As freelancers, it is very important to build your portfolio to attract more work and new clients. A good project for a good client will get you more interesting work and better pay in the future. You will be making more money down the line, keep that in mind when you consider which project to take on.

To that point, try not to cut your current contract short or bail on a current project if something more exciting come along. If you have to do it, try giving your current client plenty of notice to avoid leaving on a bad term. Being a freelancer does not exempt you from acting professionally. People will not hire you back if you leave a bad impression.

Lastly, never work for free. As young designers, you will inevitably run into people who ask you to do spec work in exchange for exposure or promise for future work. While it might be tempting, do not entertain that idea. Most likely, these people are also doing this to other creatives as well to collect work. If they care about the quality of the work and your talent, they would respect you enough to not ask you to do work for free. And it is not just small and private clients that are doing this. I interviewed with a relatively well-known publication, the interviewer asked me to do a 'design assignment' to test my skills. When I politely declined, the interviewer told me that it is a mandatory part of the interview process, and I would not be considered for next steps. This is larger issue with the creative industry as a whole. It happens to designers, photographers, illustrators, fashion designers, you name it. And creatives allow that to happen by not educating ourselves about the value of our work. Doctors and electricians get paid for their time and effort, so should we. If we all stop agreeing to work for free, this attitude toward creatives will eventually change for the better." **Long Vu, Freelance Art Director/Designer, Brooklyn, New York**

Money

Freelancing has ups and downs. Some months you might be fully booked on steady work, and other months might leave you wondering when you're going to see the next paycheck. Before you start freelancing full-time, it's smart to start taking on a few freelance projects while you're employed full time. Make sure you have at least six months of living expenses saved up.

Freelancing and taxes

As a freelancer, you need to manage your taxes. The IRS (Internal Revenue Service) requires quarterly estimated taxes from anyone freelancing, so it's important to pre-pay your taxes on a quarterly basis. For more details, visit www.irs.gov.

Some invoice apps that you can use to easily track your freelance income for taxes:

> Harvest
> Freshbooks
> QuickBooks

As a freelancer, you'll also need to figure out how to price yourself. There are several ways of pricing your services:

> Hourly rate
> Day rate
> Weekly rate
> Project-based fee

Website to calculate rates:

> Whatismydayrate.com

166

Ask the professionals: Money matters

Managing money and finances as a freelancer

How do you manage your money as a freelancer?

"I hired a tax preparer to help with taxes. It was only a few hundred dollars and made sure that I was filling out my tax forms properly. It was a whole lot less stressful than worrying if I was doing it correctly. I also keep track of every invoice and details of the project in a spreadsheet online so that at the end of the year I can make sure I'm not missing any forms." **Sam Stringer-Hye, Senior Designer, Publicis Sapient, Brooklyn, New York**

"Everyone says this, and it's true, have a 6 month safety net before you start. It might take a while for hirers to learn who you are and then for a project to line up right.

Put at least half (more than half if you can) of every check away for taxes and retirement. Then put the max ($5,500) into a Roth IRA. Financial planning services like Charles Schwab other 401k options, use these or any other tax free retirement program to save and put in as much as you can.

Find a good financial planner or accountant to consult with. I'm extremely fortunate in that this person for me is my Dad. But if he wasn't able to help me with this, I would have had to find a third party to help as I would have been lost.

Start an LLC and open a business account associated with it (or at the very least a separate account in your name). There are some places that prefer to pay you as a vendor, so having an LLC is just good to have. Having a business account that you put your tax money and savings into just makes it easier. Also, if you keep a little bit extra in it for making business expenses, it makes it easier to track and write off when you go to do your taxes.

If you happen to have a family member or friend who can give you financial or business advice, discuss it over a meal. . . then pay for the meal and write it off as a business expense." **Michael Mitzman, Freelance Designer & Art Director, Brooklyn, New York**

"I believe one of the most important things you need to learn aside from honing your craft, is financial literacy. Being self-employed, your income can vary drastically month to month, so you need to have a budget and stay on top of your finances. Use a budgeting app (mint, YNAB, etc.), learn how to make contracts, set aside 30–40% for taxes, and figure out if operating as a sole proprietor or S-Corp or LLC works best for you. There are many books available that can help you with this as well. Another piece of advice is to plan for the future. Build an emergency fund for 3–6 months of expenses as well as funding a retirement account (this could help you save taxes as well)." **Tyler Wergin, Freelance Designer and Animator, New York, New York**

"I do my design work through an LLC and have a separate business bank account and credit card for my expenses. Even though I'm currently a single person entity, I find it easier and cleaner to keep my finances apart from my personal costs.

I use QuickBooks for my invoices and expense tracking. I'm mindful of keeping all of the receipts my business expenses (monthly subscriptions, Ubers for business meetings, etc.). As a independent contractor there are a number of tax deductions that apply so I recommend working with a good accountant.

I've also read a few books on how to set up my business and finances. My favorite is *The Business Side of Creativity* by Cameron S. Foote. I actually read it before I started freelancing and I suggest reading it if you're serious about taking that step." **Amanda R. George, Senior Design Lead, Huge, Brooklyn, New York**

"I wish I can say I use fancy software, but that's not the case. I keep record of my projects and my money on a simple spreadsheet where I create columns for: Client/Project/Cost/Type of Payment/Month/Status/1099 or W2/Tax form/Tax %. So the idea of that simple format is to track my projects, how much money I'm making, which months are the most active (you can get a better sense of this through the years when you compare them) and also how much money from each project is left after taxes. I start this form in early January and every time I finish a project, I fill out my form, also I have another spreadsheet where I track all my expenses of my studio: Transport, Materials/Tools, Trips, Studio Rent, meetings and so on. If you organize your finances, it's easy to know if you are doing well or if you have to push yourself a bit more to get what you want." **Cristian Vargas, Designer and Associate Creative Director, Brooklyn, New York**

"As a freelancer, getting new projects and clients is crucial, but that by itself is not enough to make your freelance career viable. Freelancing comes with the responsibility of managing business expenses, organizing receipts, tracking down your clients for late payment. Having a solid understanding of how finance works is key to any successful business, and this cannot be more true with freelancing.

A mistake many new freelancers make is they often fail to keep track of their expenses and receipts, which will come back and haunt them when tax season comes around. Another mistake is underestimating your tax liability. Screwing up on your taxes could easily ruin your entire year, you may end up playing catch-up on the taxes you owe. To avoid such situation, you should:

Set a budget, live within your means. Anticipate your income, and calculate your expenses for the quarter. From there, you can figure out the minimum baseline on how much money you can spend.

Always set aside enough money to pay taxes.

Find an accountant/CPA whom you feel comfortable with to help you understand how to structure your finance.

Get yourself in the habit of collecting receipts and organize them into categories such as travel, meal, equipment, etc.. . . Your accountant will thank you.

Some of useful tools for managing your finance:

QuickBooks Online: this app allows you to keep track of your business income and spending. You can generate, send, and track invoices; the best part of this invoicing feature is that it shows you how many times the person viewed your invoice(s). There is a subscription fee for this app, but the benefits really out-weight the cost.

Expense tracking apps: there are many apps available on both iOS and Androids that allow you to upload and organize your receipts. Some credit cards offer features to attach receipt images to your transactions online.

Get yourself a credit card dedicated for business expenses: this is really optional, but having all of your business-related expenses under the same card makes things a lot easier to manage.

Considering opening saving accounts: freelancing means that you do not have the benefits of 401k contributions like full-time staff. There are retirement saving accounts that you can open to start accumulate. You can continue contributing to these accounts even if you decide to go on staff somewhere." **Long Vu, Freelance Art Director/Designer, Brooklyn, New York**

How do you figure out how to price yourself?

"Pricing yourself is difficult because there are many factors involved. Size of the business, excitement about the project, experience level. But ultimately don't sell yourself short because you're only hurting yourself down the road. Ask around, I find more people are willing to talk about their rates than not and it helps you discover what companies are willing to pay." **Sam Stringer-Hye, Senior Designer, Publicis Sapient, Brooklyn, New York**

"Talk to other freelancers of similar levels and just ask what they get. It might be a little awkward (and they might exaggerate their actual rate), but it'll help for you to get a range.

The more projects you bring in, you'll start to get a feeling for what you can get. Different sized clients and projects have different budgets and it's all about what a project is worth to you.

The smaller, lower budget ones, are usually more fun and make for better portfolio pieces. So sometimes you have to look at it as an investment on your part since those pieces will bring in more work.

I will say a few things regarding specifics:

I tend to stay away from working on pitches, but if I do get talked into working on one, I charge almost double my regular rate (it's still almost never worth it).

Price out weekly rates for at least six days of work. Weekly rates are usually a way to screw you into working weekends (I'd also advise to stay away from these in general).

Companies like Google and Apple pay well, but it's pretty competitive with everyone else. The companies that pay the most are the evil ones (pharma, cable, oil, etc.). Stick to your morals, but if you do get approached by one of these and need the work, take them to the bank then donate some of your check to a charity to combat them. It won't completely make up for what you've done, but it'll make you feel a little bit better about it. Not that I've ever done anything like this before." **Michael Mitzman, Freelance Designer & Art Director, Brooklyn, New York**

"There are many aspects involved when it comes to pricing for a job. Know what duties are being asked of you. During the initial contact from a client or studio, I always ask for a brief to help understand not only what the project is about, but if I am even a right fit for the job. To help me figure out my rates when I first started,

I sought out as many people as I could to see what a reasonable rate was for a junior designer/animator in my market (NYC). Depending on the job, you can charge a project rate, day rate, or hourly. Once I had an idea of my day rate, it helped me price out an hourly and project rate. There are also many online forums to help guide you as well. One of the most popular is 'mixed.parts'." **Tyler Wergin, Freelance Designer and Animator, New York, New York**

"Pricing yourself is a tricky thing. I've learned most of what I know from speaking with other freelancers as well as independent recruiters. Rates differ per market, design discipline (graphic design, product design, UX, etc.), years of experience and size of agency/ organization. I'd recommend joining a freelancer organization within your area and have conversations with others in the field. I know a lot of freelancers who keep that information close, but I believe that there's enough work out there for everyone and we should help one another by being transparent about what we're billing." **Amanda R. George, Senior Design Lead, Huge, Brooklyn, New York**

"After more than 15 years, I am reminded that there is not a single rule that applies to a company or position. I think you have to start by looking at annual salary guides, for example Coroflot Design Salary Guide, in the design industry, but use it as just a reference point. Build your career slowly, never get underpaid and as soon as you get more experience and more skills, ask for more. In general, I try to push my rate a bit up (just a bit) every year. coroflot.com/designsalaryguide" **Cristian Vargas, Designer and Associate Creative Director, Brooklyn, New York**

"Pricing yourself is never straightforward, especially when you just start making your transition into freelancing. Even experienced freelancers are uncertain of how much they should charge for each project due to many different factors that go in determining your rate, namely:

Your experience: as in most professions, the more experience you have, the more money you can ask. While there are exceptions to the rules, students and juniors should expect to be on the lower end of the scale.

Your work: If your work stands out in the crowd, not only that you would be able to land more gigs, clients will be more inclined to be flexible with their budgets in order to secure a contract with you. A well-presented portfolio makes a big difference.

Your specialty: different types of design work are priced differently. For example, Illustrators' work generally require more time, and the process is unique to each person; therefore, it makes more sense for them to charge a project rate rather than an hourly rate like a designer. Even within the visual design discipline, branding designers get different hourly rates than editorial designers.

Your client: A well-funded startup or a large corporation can afford to pay more for the same type of work compared to smaller/private clients because their budgets are larger. Oftentimes, freelancers set their on-going rate based off of the average rate they have been getting from previous assignments/clients.

As a start, establish an ideal scenario—a baseline rate that you need to get in order to make your freelance career viable. First, calculate a yearly figure that you need to earn in order to afford your living costs. Make sure that figure includes all the expenses such as rent, equipment, healthcare, etc. . . . Divide that figure by the number of weeks you are expecting to work a year. Then divide that by 40 to get your hourly rate. Be realistic with yourself, you likely won't be working all year-round; so remember to account that into the equation when you consider how many weeks you should be expecting to work. In short, your total earning needs to carry you through the downtime.

To summarize, my formula would look something like this:

Desired yearly income ÷ 46 (weeks) ÷ 40 (hours) = Hourly rate

Once you have set a rate that you feel met those requirements, use that to start the negotiations with your potential clients; they will likely tell you whether your rate is within their range or not. Being flexible with your rate allows you to be more competitive; at the same time, do not sell yourself short. Based on how the market responds over time, you can set the high and low ends of your ongoing rate.

One tool that I find useful is this questionnaire by the NuSchool (http://thenuschool.com/how-much/#/ start). By answering a few questions regarding the project, this tool gives you a ballpark of how much you should charge for the project.

Another good reference is the *Graphic Artist Guild Handbook*: this annually published handbook is free for members of the Guild, but it can also be purchased on Amazon. It breaks down hourly rate by each design professions, from illustrators to web producers. As a bonus, they include sample contracts in the book, which is incredibly useful to reference." **Long Vu, Art Director & Designer, Brooklyn, New York**

Self-promotion

Success in freelancing depends on ruthless self-promotion. Who you know will get you in the door. What you know will keep you there. Once you decide you're ready to make a transition to freelance, update your LinkedIn profile to "freelance," and email your contacts to let them know you're available for work. Network with your existing contacts to find gigs. You might consider tapping your immediate network, cold emails, and meeting up for coffee or lunches.

Other methods for promoting yourself are to create profiles on websites where recruiters might be searching for freelancers.

Websites for promoting yourself

- Working Not Working
- Upwork
- LinkedIn

Ask the professionals: Promotion

Insights from professional freelancers on the importance of self-promotion

What's the most important advice in promoting yourself?

"Take the time to really think about the work you've done and the decisions you made putting into it. During my full-time career I never had to think about the reason behind my design decisions. It made it hard to talk about my work and to be critical of myself. Ultimately that hurt me when building my portfolio or when clients asked about projects I had worked on. I have learned so much in the last 2 years and now I am much better at describing the work in a way that convinces the client that I know what I'm doing. It also means that I am advocating for not only my own instinctual taste, but to tell clients that I have their best interests in mind." **Sam Stringer-Hye, Senior Designer, Publicis Sapient, Brooklyn, New York**

"The biggest thing for promoting myself has just been staying in contact with people I've worked with before. I have a spreadsheet of contact info and I'll send out an email if I have a new project live or if I know I'll have upcoming availability. If I see on LinkedIn, someone has a new job, I'll send a note congratulating them. For me, it's just about staying fresh in people's head.

The one mistake I've made (and continue to make) is not promoting myself on social media or entering award shows. Instagram and Dribble are great ways to interact with other designers and promote your work. I'm constantly admiring and liking other designer's work, but for some unexplained reason, I'm horrible about promoting mine.

The same goes for award shows. I know this is a more controversial topic, and I personally have no feelings on it one way or the other, but they are a great way to promote and get your work out there (plus adding those to your resume always looks nice). It's another opportunity that I'm missing out for unexplained reasons (it's a fear of rejection)." **Michael Mitzman, Freelance Designer & Art Director, Brooklyn, New York**

"Self-promotion is a highly valuable tool that can help you acquire new business. Using social media platforms can help you get comfortable posting work as well giving you a voice. Building a website of your portfolio is key. Make sure that you're only posting the work you're proud of, as well as the work you want to do. It's better to have fewer, more meaningful projects than a plethora of mediocre work. Self-promotion is actually an aspect that I struggle with the most, I am very critical of the work I do and tend to not showcase as much as I probably should." **Tyler Wergin, Freelance Designer and Animator, New York, New York**

"Change things and stop to try to be like the others to fit in. Go out there and try something different, even if you don't get 'likes,' because design and life is about being real and showing your uniqueness. You need to find a balance between new social media digital tools to promote yourself, but please do not forget that the world was amazing before internet and smartphones." **Cristian Vargas, Designer and Associate Creative Director, Brooklyn, New York**

"As a young designer, you probably have favorite designer(s) that you admire, and chances are their work is highly visible across the web and printed publications. You probably wondered how they got to where they are. While you might think that these designers' work were 'discovered' and featured, that is only partially true. It's In order for your work to get noticed, you must proactively promote them.

There are numerous award bodies, communities, and online publications that showcase the best creative work in the industry. Some are more specialized than others; for example, awwwards and FWA focus on digital work. On the other hand, Eyes on Design by AIGA is more focus on general graphic design and branding. Design blogs, online magazines, portfolio platforms like Behance and Dribble are free; most of you probably is already using these platforms for inspirations. Their curators comb through hundreds of new entries each day to select projects they find compelling to feature. These sites have high traffic, so if your work get featured, it will be seen by thousands. Given the amount of submissions, it is very competitive. Make sure your case studies is polished, easy-to-digest, and comprehensive before you submit.

The more prestige awards have submission fees, which is the main barrier-to-entry for most freelancers. Those fees range from $35 and up, they can add up quickly if you consider submitting to multiple awards. Do not let that discourage you, if you really believe in your work, take the risk and submit it. Even if you don't win, you still receive the exposure and attention from professionals in the field. One award I definitely recommend young creatives to apply for is the Art Director Club Young Guns, an annual award for creatives under 30 years of age. It is an incredibly tough award, you are not only competing against other designers, you are competing against writers, directors, photographers. Majority of the winners' freelance careers took off after they have been selected as Young Guns; big artist reps always stay on top of this award to find new talent to add to their rosters.

Lastly, lots of recruiters find talent using Linkedin, Working not Working, etc. . . . Don't be afraid to reach out to recruiters and introduce yourself, if they like your work, they will try to set you up for future job or freelance opportunities. So make sure your portfolio and profile are up-to-date. We are living in the age of information overload, it is easier than ever to put your work up online, at the same time, the amount of design work floating on the Internet is overwhelming. If you don't reach out to people and bring your work to their attention, you are missing out on potential opportunities. I have had multiple recruiters reaching out to me years after we made the first introduction." **Long Vu, Art Director & Designer, Brooklyn, New York**

171

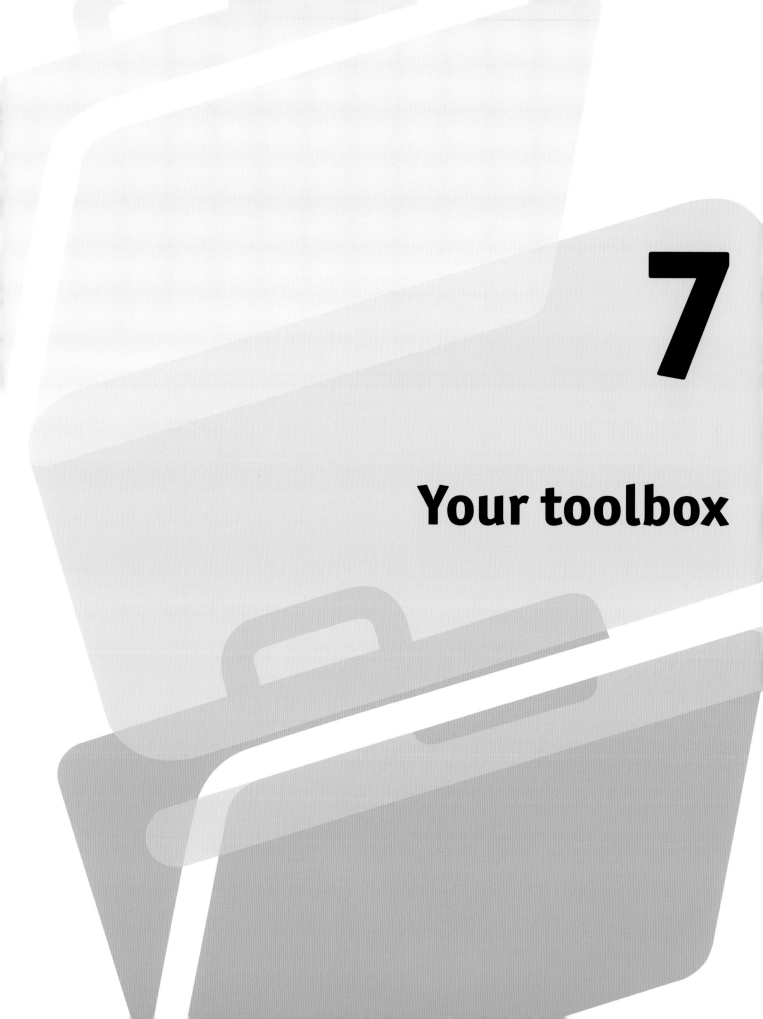

7

Your toolbox

This section is a quick go-to reference guide that you can use throughout your career. This section will include easy-to-follow templates for applying for a job/thank you/follow-ups, cover letters, accepting/declining an offer, as well as setting up informal interviews with prospective clients/employers to review your portfolio (not necessarily in response to a particular job post).

Templates

These templates are meant to be used as guides.
Add your own words and personalize each template
for the best results.

APPLYING FOR A JOB

Dear [Name],

I'm applying for the [Position name] at [Company] because [reason].

Some of my favorite projects [Company] has produced are [name some of your favorite projects and write why]. It's work like this, that gets me excited about the opportunity to join the team at [Company].

Attached is my cover letter and my portfolio.

I would love a chance to come in for an interview to hear about the opportunity at [Company]. My contact information is [contact]. Looking forward to hearing from you.

Thank you,

[Your name]

APPLYING FOR AN INTERNSHIP AFTER MEETING AT AN INDUSTRY EVENT

Dear [Name],

I wanted to thank you for such a great night. All of the feedback and tips you shared were very helpful. I am very interested in an internship opportunity with [Company]. I've attached copy of my resume and a PDF of my portfolio. Please let me know if I can provide you with any more information.

Thank you again! I look forward to hearing from you.

Best,

[Your name]

COVER LETTERS

Dear [Name],

The first time I visited [Company], I was on a school trip with my undergraduate design program. I remember feeling inspired by the work with Google. My passion for product design, user experience, apps, and my experience in digital make me an ideal candidate. When I learned that [Company] is hiring a Junior Designer, this was a perfect opportunity for me to apply and contribute to a company who believes in delighting the user with seamless user experience.

I interned as a product design intern at [Company], a digital ad agency in Summer 2017, as a part of the [name of the team or project], helping to launch a new responsive website. I gained the experience in collaborating with other designers, as well as engineers, copywriters, and strategists. Through my previous design internship, I learned how to be a team player: interacting with people of various interests and backgrounds, and confidently sharing my thoughts to fellow team members.

I believe that digital design can connect with users' emotions through the interaction between technology and us. Additionally, I am the Editor of my university's design blog, where I contribute weekly articles. I want to work at [Company] because I am inspired to learn that [Company] publishes regular design articles on Medium. I live and breathe design, and I am confident that I can make a difference at [Company].

Please see the attached resume for my qualifications. Additionally, my portfolio can be viewed at [URL].

I look forward to speaking with you. I can be reached at [phone number] and [email]. Thank you for your time and consideration.

Sincerely,

[Your name]

THANK YOU AFTER INTERVIEW

Variation 1

Hi [Name],

I wanted to thank you for your time. It was truly a pleasure to meet you at [Company].

[Projects you discussed] is an opportunity that I am eager to work on with you and the team.

I am really looking forward to hearing from [Company] and [try to add something personal from the interview].

Yours,

[Your name]

175

THANK YOU AFTER INTERVIEW

Variation 2

Hi [Name],

Thank you so much for your time on Friday. I really enjoyed meeting you and especially appreciate your transparency during the interview. Feedback is what helps me grow and I definitely thrive in environments that are direct. I just wish we had more time to discuss [particular project], but I'm glad we got everything working by the end. Everyone else I met during the interview was awesome as well, I admire the experience and culture of the [Company] team. Thanks again and I hope you to hear from you soon.

Sincerely,

[Your name]

THANK YOU AFTER INTERVIEW

Variation 3

Dear [Name],

Thank you so much for meeting with me and letting me present my work last Friday. It was a pleasure to meet you, and to receive your professional design advice.

I'm very enthusiastic about the possibility of joining [Company] and hope to work on amazing projects with you and the team.

Looking forward to hearing from you in the near future.

Best,

[Your name]

THANK YOU AFTER INTERVIEW, IF YOU WANT TO CLARIFY A QUESTION

For example, the internship interview went well, but you stumbled on the last question, when someone asked you "what makes you unique." As fate would hold it, as soon as you left the interview, you had the perfect answer! What should you do? Here is a template that you could use.

Dear [Name],

Thank you so much for taking the time to interview me today. I thought more about your final question after we parted ways, and wanted to share my answer to your final question: What makes me memorable compared to the other design candidates?

I'm memorable because I have a positive, lively personality that makes people enjoy working with me. When combined with the three essential characteristics of a successful intern (listed below), my passion for advertising shines.

Collaborative: I enjoy being involved in clubs, organizations, and group projects where I not only work with others but take the lead to produce great work even on tight deadlines.

Communicative: Through my agency internship experiences, I've learned to relay client feedback to members of my team in a constructive manner.

Eager to learn: Whether it's studying abroad in two different cultures, reading every industry blog, or listening to new podcasts (thanks for the suggestion!), I love to learn new things and grow.

Taken together, I am a person that loves to tackle new challenges, has a positive outlook, and gets the job done. I know that when you meet me in person you'll see that I am a perfect fit for this position, and the position is perfect for me.

Sincerely,

[Your name]

THANK YOU AFTER INTERVIEW, YOU WANT TO KEEP IN TOUCH WITH THE PERSON

Dear [Name],

It was nice connecting with you yesterday! Thank you for your time to interview me and giving me the details of the internship program. I really appreciate your offer to chat after the interview.

Whether I end up at [Company] or not, I would really love to reconnect with you to learn more about your perspective on advertising and design.

Please let me know if you have any questions and I look forward to hearing back from you soon.

Best regards,

[Your name]

FOLLOW-UPS (YOU HAVEN'T HEARD AFTER INTERVIEWS)

Hi [Name],

I'm following up regarding the [Position] at [Company]. I enjoyed coming in and meeting [names of the people you met] to discuss the potential opportunity on the [projects that you discussed].

I'm excited about the opportunity and believe that my skills in design and presentation would bring value to the growing design team.

Please let me know if you have any questions or need a copy of my resume, or additional samples of my work.

Best,

[Your name]

ACCEPTING AN OFFER

Hi [Name],

Thank you for extending the offer. I am thrilled to join the team! Attached is my signed offer letter. Please let me know if you need any additional paperwork. Looking forward to starting at [Company] on [start date].

Thank you,

[Your name]

DECLINING AN OFFER

Hi [Name],

I am incredibly grateful for your help and for the opportunity to meet the team. The [Position] at [Company] is an incredible opportunity, but unfortunately, I decided to pursue [state the reason why you're declining the offer].

I would be happy to speak over the phone with you, but wanted to send you a note as well. I appreciate the time and energy the team dedicated to meeting with me.

With gratitude,

[Your name]

ASKING TO SET UP INFORMAL INTERVIEWS (NOT NECESSARILY IN RESPONSE TO A PARTICULAR JOB POST)

Example Email:

Hi [Name],

I recently finished updating my portfolio and wanted to get feedback on it before starting my job search in [industry]. I was wondering about is [describe exactly what feedback you're looking for]. Could you please review my portfolio and share your feedback by [date]? I'd love to get your honest opinion and advice. My portfolio url is [url].

Thank you,

[Your name]

8

Appendix

Professional organizations

The following is a list of professional organizations to join while you're still a student (or shortly after graduating). Joining professional graphic design associations will allow you a great opportunity to network at chapter events. These professionals can lead you to an internship or a job opening. Many professional design organizations offer reduced joining fees to students. You can also ask about volunteer opportunities in exchange for free event admission.

American Institute of Graphic Arts (AIGA)—check your local chapter
Art Directors Club
D&AD
Fabrica
Industrial Designers Society of America (IDSA)
Society for Experiential Graphic Design
Society of Illustrators
Spark Design Professionals
The Cradle to Cradle Products Innovation Institute
The Design Management Institute (DMI)
The International Interior Design Association (IIDA)
The One Club
The Society of Typographic Aficionados (SOTA)
Type Directors Club
United Adworkers

Sample questions to ask when you're networking

Where do you work?
What do you do?
How long have you worked at [company]?
How do you like it there?
What kind of projects do you work on?
What's your favorite part of [company]?
How did you get hired at [company]?
What's the work environment like?
What's your day to day?

Quick tips for creating a portfolio

Curate Your Work
Go for Variety
Invest in Photography
Write about your work
Keep It Current

Money

Shouldiworkforfree.com
Coroflot Design Salary Guide

Website hosting/sites

Squarespace
Semplice Labs
Cargo
WIX

Online design education

General Assembly
Skillshare
Lynda.com
CodeCademy
Coursera

Design Inspiration

UnderConsideration:
underconsideration.com

Brand New:
underconsideration.com/brandnew
Corporate and brand identity.

Art of the Menu:
underconsideration.com/artofthemenu
Print trends, menu layouts from all over the world, color usage. Not your typical diner menus on this site.

Quipsologies:
underconsideration.com/quipsologies

FPO:
underconsideration.com/fpo
Tons of resumes, business cards, card stock.

Swissmiss:
swiss-miss.com
Has a cool weekly Friday link pack, just cool things that happen in the world, most related to design, some not.

Bestfolio:
bestfolios.com
View portfolio website, case study, and resume design examples.

But-t-er-ick's Prac-ti-cal Ty-pog-ra-phy:
practicaltypography.com
Typography rules.

Adobe Cloud:
adobe.com/creativecloud.html

Typography Resources

Typography.com
Adobe Fonts
Thinking with Type by Ellen Lupton—for grid basics and type basics
Type Foundries

Recommended Type Foundries

- Colophon Foundry
- Commercial Type
- FontShop
- Grilli Type
- Hoefler & Co.
- Klim Type Foundry
- Lineto
- Linotype
- Monotype
- Optimo
- Swiss Typefaces
- TypeNetwork

Freelancing Resources

YNAB (You Need a Budget)app:
youneedabudget.com/our-app-lineup

Mint app:
mint.com

QuickBooks—for invoices and expense tracking:
quickbooks.intuit.com

The Business Side of Creativity by Cameron S. Foote

Other good books to get started in your career
Bird by Bird: Some Instructions on Writing and Life by Anne Lamott—for writing

Contributor biographies

Amanda R. George
Senior Design Lead
Huge
Brooklyn, New York
amandageorge.com
linkedin.com/in/amandageorge1
hugeinc.com

Amanda George is a New York based creative specializing in design and brand/marketing strategy. She has over a decade of experience with projects that range from designing commerce experiences and brand identities for Nike to developing media plans and strategies across Campbell's diverse portfolio of food and beverages.

Outside of design, she has a passion for bakeries and can be found roaming the streets of Brooklyn in search of a vegan cookie.

Anna Rising
Designer & Illustrator
Oslo, Norway
Class of 2015, BFA Graphic Design, The University of the Arts, Philadelphia, Pennsylvania
annarising.com
instagram.com/annarising
behance.net/annarising
dribbble.com/annarising
linkedin.com/in/annamrising

Anna Rising is an American-born graphic designer and illustrator currently living in Oslo, Norway. With a diverse background spanning across digital, print, and branding, she is passionate about creating holistic visual systems that are fresh and culturally relevant. Before moving to Oslo, Anna lived in New York City where she worked with clients including Google, Anheuser-Busch, M&M's, Budlight, and HuffPost. Aside from design, Anna enjoys chai lattes, ocean documentaries, petting other people's dogs, and spontaneous solo trips to new countries.

Cristian Vargas
Designer & Associate Creative Director
Brooklyn, New York
typozon.com
linkedin.com/in/typozon
instagram.com/typozon

I'm a dreamer, urban cyclist, amateur fashion and accessories designer who loves and gets inspired by nature. I'm also a graphic and typeface designer with more than 16 years of experience crafting the visual voice for companies, products, and Individuals.

Currently running my own design studio Typozon®, and working as a freelance Designer & Associate Creative Director for multiple companies in New York City, in my spare time I teach typography and calligraphy.

Danielle Song
Talent Operations Coordinator
Huge
Brooklyn, New York
hugeinc.com
daniellesong.com

Danielle is all about building systems and process at Huge. She hails from the Bay Area, the land of the eternal fall, and can't stand humid summers. On weekends you can find her drawing at cafes and carrying around her film camera but forgetting to take photos.

Ein Jung
Product Designer, Bunch, New York, New York
Class of 2018, BFA Advertising and Design, School of Visual Arts, New York, New York
einjung.work
*instagram.com/ein_ein_*
linkedin.com/in/einjung

Ein is a creative thinker and maker based in New York City. She completed her BFA in Advertising and Design from the School of Visual Arts. Though she was born in Korea, she spent a majority of her life in India—up in the foothills of the Himalayan mountains. After working at R/GA and Google Creative Lab, she is currently at a startup called Bunch as a Product Designer.

From the initial brief to the final product, Ein enjoys all the in-between workings of creating something thoughtful and beautiful. Her main focuses lie in user experience/interface design and branding.

When Ein's not staring into computer screens, she spends most of her time taking photos on 35mm film, playing Zelda, or throwing pots on the wheel. She is also a full-time cat mom to a three-legged rescue named Eileen.

Elena Anderson
Recruitment & Operations Manager
ustwo, New York, New York
ustwo.com

Elena didn't know what she wanted to do after college and found herself in various operational roles. Over time, she realized that what motivated her most was working with and understanding the people around her. Fast forward a few years and she is thrilled to have found a way to utilize her passion for people to connect with great talent across the globe.

Emily Wengert
Group Vice President, User Experience
Huge
Brooklyn, New York
hugeinc.com
emilywengert.com

Emily Wengert is Group Vice President for User Experience at Huge, focused on integrated retail and ecommerce relationships. Since joining Huge she has driven customer experience design and digital transformation initiatives for companies including Target, Comcast, SK-II, Google, Gucci, and Loblaws. Prior to Huge, Emily led creative teams at Digitas and worked as a journalist. She received a bachelor's degree in English from the College of William and Mary. Her favorite side project is raising two strong girls, who manage to surprise her and make her belly laugh on a daily basis.

Fred Saldanha
Global Chief Creative Officer
VMLY&R
vmlyr.com

Fred recently joined VMLY&R from Arnold, where he helped the agency achieve its best results at Cannes in the last 15 years. Fred's global perspective comes from nearly 30 years of experience working in markets such as Lisbon, London, São Paulo, New York, and Boston. He has spent time at agencies like Y&R, DDB, FCB, Grey, W+K, Ogilvy, and Isobar, where he served as CCO for the Americas. In the US, Fred has spent the last five years between Brooklyn and Boston. He was behind the first Super Bowl spot for Huge, which led to Quicken Loans best sales day ever. He has collected over 40 Cannes Lions among other awards like D&AD, One Show, Webbys, LIA, and Clio.

Gail Anderson
Chair, BFA Design and BFA Advertising
Creative Director, Visual Arts Press
School of Visual Arts
New York, New York

behance.net/gailycurl5504
Gailycurl.com
vap.sva.edu

Gail Anderson is a NYC-based designer, educator, and writer. She is Chair of BFA Design and BFA Advertising at the School of Visual Arts, and the creative director at Visual Arts Press. Anderson has served as senior art director at *Rolling Stone*, creative director of design at SpotCo, and as a designer at The Boston Globe Sunday Magazine and Vintage Books. She has taught at SVA for close to thirty years and has co-authored 15 books on design, typography, and illustration with the fabulous Steven Heller. Anderson serves on the Citizens' Stamp Advisory Committee for the US Postal Service and the advisory board of Poster House. She is an AIGA Medalist and the 2018 recipient of the Cooper Hewitt, Smithsonian Lifetime Achievement Award for Design. Her work is represented in the permanent collections of the Library of Congress, the Milton Glaser Design Archives, and the National Museum of African American History and Culture.

Hieu Tran
Product Designer
OpenSpace
San Francisco, California
Class of 2016, MFA Graphic Design, Maryland Institute College of Art, Baltimore, Maryland
hieutran.co
twitter.com/hieutran42
instagram.com/hieutran42
linkedIn.com/in/hieutran42
dribbble.com/hieutran42
behance.net/hieutran42

Hieu Tran is a Product Designer at OpenSpace, SF. He was born in Indonesia, grew up in Saigon, immigrated to the United States at the age of 11, and now parties in San Francisco. He graduated from the Johns Hopkins University with a BA in Computer Science and Cognitive Science, and then from the Maryland Institute College of Art with an MFA in Graphic Design. Maybe once he is debt-free, he will pursue a PhD in something cool. He particularly enjoys working with grids, fucking up letterforms with a scanner, taking dangerous photos, laughing at designer jokes, dancing when no one is watching, and drinking cheap wine from Trader Joe's.

Hieu used to specialize in editorial, branding, and information visualization. He particularly enjoys working with big and small data, transforming content from 2D to 3D, and exploring the social and cultural impact of digital communication and social media. And while he still loves to do these things—he is slowly making his way into digital product and interaction design by working on more web and app projects with a strong focus on UX strategy, prototyping, and user testing.

Hieu tries to not take himself very seriously and always tries to be a rebel. He thinks that professionalism is overrated and that people should be themselves as long as the work gets done.

Ida Woldemichael
Associate Creative Director
Wide Eye
Washington D.C.
idawoldemichael.com

Ida Woldemichael is a creative director with over 12 years of design experience. The heart of her work is design for political activism, and branding. Her work spans from design with top-tier agencies to notable non-profit organizations including: Brooklyn Children's Museum, the Clinton Foundation, Hillary for America, NYC Votes, and USAID.

Ida received her Master of Fine Arts degree, in Graphic Design, from the Maryland Institute College of Art; and her Bachelor of Fine Arts degree from Virginia Tech. Ida served as a lead designer on the historic presidential campaign for Hillary Clinton, developing the popular supporter tagline, "I'm with her."

She is currently an Associate Creative Director at Wide Eye, an educator at NYU, and on AIGA NY's board of directors.

Ilgin Sezer
Associate Creative Director
Huge
New York, New York
hugeinc.com
ilginsezer.com

I'm an Associate Creative Director at Huge, where I specialize using design thinking to create digital products and services deeply rooted in the brand story. Recent work I led or contributed to includes development of design systems, corporate communications and spatial experiences for companies like Google, IBM, Accenture and Vanguard. In my free time I like to dabble in ceramics and metal smithing, go hiking, and read sci-fi.

Jason Fujikuni
Art Director, Brand Identity
The New York Times
New York, New York
Class of 2017, BFA Graphic Design, Rhode Island School of Design, Providence, Rhode Island
jasonfujikuni.com
instagram.com/jasonfujikuni

Jason Fujikuni is an art director at *The New York Times*. Jason works on the brand identity design team to develop identities, systems and style guides for cross-platform use in the newsroom and company. In his spare time, he volunteers with the youth ministry at his church.

Jason is a designer by profession and an artist at heart, a nomadic Angelino and a reclusive New Yorker, a son, a brother, and a friend.

Jeffrey Betts
Experience Designer
Responsify
Brooklyn, NY
responsify.com
jeffreybetts.me

I craft user-focused and seamless experiences. I have both a design and engineering background, which has enabled me to work in a hybrid role and rapidly iterate on new ideas. Currently I'm working at Responsify as an Experience Designer. I graduated from Farmingdale State College with a degree in Visual Communications, where I focused on UI/UX design and software development. I love photography and to travel. Many of my photos are available for free on FOCA at https://focastock.com/.

Julia Whitley
Graphic Designer
Fenix Design Studio
Kansas City, Missouri
Class of 2017, BFA Graphic Design, Oklahoma State University, Stillwater, Oklahoma
julialwhitley.com
instagram.com/juliawhitley
instagram.com/stuffbyjules
linkedIn.com/in/juliawhitley1

Julia Whitley is a Graphic Designer at Fenix Design Studio in Kansas City, Missouri. She was born in Tulsa, Oklahoma and lives in Kansas City. She graduated from Oklahoma State University with a BFA in Graphic Design in 2017. Her primary medium is print and she has done work for clients such as IHOP, Applebees, Big Brothers Big Sisters, as well as some local brands. She has art directed food photography, developed social strategy and execution, and created packaging design. She loves taking a brand, rethinking their strategy and creating a design system around that strategy. Julia loves throwing pottery and making useful wares for her home and friends. She will also almost always be seen wearing stripes and has a cat named Brinkley who takes up most of her time, money, and photo storage.

Julia Zeltser
Creative Director & Partner
Hyperakt
Brooklyn, New York
Hyperakt.com

Julia is a founding Partner and Creative Director at Hyperakt. Her keen eye has been critical in establishing Hyperakt's visual voice and has resulted in brilliant designs for clients such as Unicef, Gotham Writers, Ford Foundation, and Malala Fund. She exhibits rigorous discipline as well as cheerful humor, making her a sharp creative, a savvy entrepreneur, and nurturing mentor. Julia initiated and leads Lunch Talks at Hyperakt, a monthly event to ignite collaboration and idea-sharing among the design community. She graduated from Parsons The New School of Design in New York and has received design accolades from organizations such as Society of Illustrators, Communication Arts, Brand New, and *How Magazine*. Born in Ukraine, Julia relocated to the United States at the age of fifteen. She lives with her husband, Lenny, her three kids, and a dog in Park Slope.

June Shin
Type Designer
Occupant Fonts/Morisawa USA
Brooklyn, New York
Class of 2017, MFA Graphic Design, Rhode Island School of Design, Providence, Rhode Island
notborninjune.com
occupantfonts.com
instagram.com/notborninjune
linkedIn.com/in/june-shin-42a10236

June Shin is a type designer, graphic designer, and educator based in New York City. After graduating from Cornell University with a BA in art history, she

studied graphic design at Parsons The New School and later at Rhode Island School of Design (RISD), where she received her master's degree and now teaches typography.

Her work is often typographically oriented, as she spends a lot of her time examining, drawing, and pondering letterforms. In addition to designing typefaces at Occupant Fonts, a brand of the Japan-based type company Morisawa, she maintains her graphic design practice, taking on freelance and self-initiated projects. Her work has been awarded by Type Directors Club, Art Directors Club, and Communication Arts, among others, featured in American and Korean publications, and exhibited internationally. On occasion, she travels to give lectures and workshops at design schools and conferences.

She currently lives in Brooklyn, New York, but works anywhere she likes. She was not born in June.

Kris Kiger
Executive Vice President, Executive Creative Director, Design
R/GA
New York, New York
rga.com

Kris leads creative teams in delivering strategy-driven brand experiences for many of the world's leading companies. Her creative leadership and skill have helped produce breakthrough work for many R/GA clients past and present—including Verizon, Samsung, Nike, L'Oréal, Walmart, and more.

She has more than 20 years of hands-on experience in working with companies to navigate the transition from the traditional business environment to the dynamic digital, mobile and social economy. Her current area of focus is helping businesses understand that "the interface is the platform of the future" and key to success in the coming era of The Internet of Things (IoT).

Kris has won virtually every award from the industry's most prestigious competitions, including the Cannes Lions, the D&AD Awards, the ANDYs, the CLIOs, and One Show Interactive. In 2008, Advertising Age named her one of their 30 "Women to Watch," a tribute honoring the industry's top female executive talent.

She received her BA in Graphic Design from the University of Arizona and lives in New York, with her husband and son.

On the weekends she can be found in the Catskills working on her side hustle of restoring and old 1938 roadside motel and tavern, the Red Rose. It's a wonderful chance to give something meaningful back to the community she and her family have spent many relaxing weekends in. It's a labor of love and from a design and branding perspective it's a chance to bring back the layers of history the place has seen over the years.

Lara McCormick
Freelance Designer
San Francisco, California
laramc.com

Lara McCormick is a nationally recognized designer, educator, and author. She gives presentations and workshops on design and typography across North America for organizations including AIGA, AdobeMAX, RGD, and TEDx. Her work has been featured in *HOW* magazine, *PRINT*, *Communication Arts*, *Graphic Design USA*, and highlighted in numerous graphic design books. She is a two-time recipient of the Sappi *Ideas that Matter* grant and a judge for Communication Arts Typography Annual (2017).

Lara received her Masters of Fine Art in Design from the School of Visual Arts, and a post-graduate degree in typography from Cooper Union. She is committed to design education, social activism, and investigating change.

Linnea Taylor
Multimedia Designer
School of Visual Arts
New York, New York
Class of 2016, BFA Design, School of Visual Arts, New York, New York
linneataylor.com
instagram.com/target__blank
linkedIn.com/in/linnea-taylor-1787198a

Linnea Taylor is a Multimedia Designer at the School of Visual Arts in New York City. She grew up on a farm in Mechanicville, New York, and moved to the city to study in the BFA Design Program at SVA, where she graduated from in 2016.

Long Vu
Art Director & Designer
Brooklyn, New York
long.vu
linkedin.com/in/long-vu-008b0518
Instagram.com/lgvu

Long Vu is an art director and designer based in Brooklyn, New York. He creates digital products, brand identities, and experiences for major and independent lifestyle, fashion, music, and culture clients. His work has been recognized and featured by *Fast Co. Innovation by Design*, Awwwards, Siteinspire, among others. Long also serves as a member of CSS Design Awards judging panel and collaborates with bands and artists on their record covers.

Lorenzo Iuculano
User Experience Designer
Think Company
Philadelphia, Pennsylvania
thinkcompany.com
lorenzoiuculano.com

Lorenzo Iuculano is a User Experience Designer for Think Company, currently living and working in Philadelphia, Pennsylvania. He was educated at Farmingdale State College of New York and trained at Huge, Brooklyn. In his free time you can find him surfing or spotting cats.

Lori Weiss
Visual Designer
Deloitte Digital
New York, New York
deloittedigital.com
lorianneweiss.com

Lori is a passionate designer who loves learning and making new discoveries in the field of graphic design. She has recently ventured into UI/UX design for virtual and augmented reality with her job at Deloitte Digital. She is a bit of a health nut and recently participated in a hackathon at work to create an app to showcase her favorite smoothie recipes.

Margaret Morales
Recruiter
Huge
Brooklyn, New York
hugeinc.com

A biology major that used to chase cheetahs in Africa, Margaret now chases creative talent in the advertising and product world. At Huge, she's digging into design and scouring the nation for top talent. When she's not working, she's playing with her rescue cat Harlem or wandering her Brooklyn neighborhood looking for the most captivating street art or dive bar band.

Masha Vainblat
Senior Digital Designer at Steven Madden, LTD
Long Island City, New York
Class of 2016, BFA Design, School of Visual Arts, New York, New York
mashavainblat.design
instagram.com/mashav
linkedin.com/in/mashavainblat

Masha Vainblat is a designer at Steve Madden with a focus on digital and e-commerce design and photo shoot art direction. She is a New York native who graduated from the School of Visual Arts with a BFA in Design in 2016.

What started as an entry level assistant position developed into a senior creative role in less than three years. Due to her persistence and ability to show her creative strengths, she was able to create a position for herself within a well established, global fashion brand.

Recognizing the importance of pursuing passion projects, Masha currently works on growing and building her crochet-wear business, Crash Crochet. She also is a new found dog lover and whenever she's not too busy laughing at her own jokes, you can find Masha eating spoonfuls of Nutella or playing beach volleyball.

Michael Mitzman
Freelance Designer & Art Director
Brooklyn, New York
mitz.nyc
linkedin.com/in/michaelmitzman
instagram.com/mmitzman
behance.net/michaelmitzman
dribbble.com/michaelmitzman

I'm an Indiana-born, Brooklyn-based designer and Art Director. I've been freelancing since 2014, and have done a variety of kinds of projects but my specialty has been digital and experience based. I also hate cheese.

Rietje Becker
Creative Director
Soulsight
Chicago, Illinois
soulsight.com
rietjebecker.com

Rietje (pronounced ree-cha) Becker is an accomplished designer, Creative Director, and type enthusiast. She specializes in corporate identity and packaging design and has worked with a variety of internationally recognized brands, such as Bayer, Mondelez, DIAGEO, CVS, Hershey's, Kraft-Heinz, Kimberly-Clark, Pepsico, and The 9/11 Memorial. Before joining Soulsight, Rietje worked at Landor, Interbrand, Sterling Brands, and Dragon Rouge. She has also taught as an adjunct professor in FIT's Packaging Design department.

When not at work, Rietje enjoys spending time with her kids, writing about design, bird watching, and things much nerdier than bird watching.

Rudy Calderon
Art Director, ESPN+
Disney Streaming Services
New York, New York
rudy.design

I am a problem solver, sightseer, and Art Director working for Disney Streaming Services in New York City. A proud graduate of Farmingdale State College. Salvadoran-American, father to an awesome little boy named Mateo, and have an awesome wifey (Hi Gaby!). I love Illustrator, Photoshop, InDesign, and Sketch. Rooftop 5v5 coed soccer champion, designer by day/ pretty decent goalkeeper by night. I have freelanced for Brooklyn Nets/Barclays Center, Miami Marlins and *Complex Magazine*. I've had the chance to hang out and photograph some pretty cool celebrities. I enjoy long podcasts, watching/playing sports, running, a really good old-fashioned, espressos, and pizza. I have A LOT of soccer jerseys. And if you've never had a Pupusa, try one, I bet you'll like it.

Ryan Scott Tandy
Product Design Manager
Instagram
San Francisco, California
instagram.com

As Product Design Manager at Instagram Ryan Scott drives creation and communication projects, most notably Instagram Stories and Instagram Direct. Working with some of the brightest minds and strongest designers, his teams deliver world renowned product experiences to over a billion global users.

With 20 years experience across several industries Ryan Scott Tandy has worn many hats as a creative; some graphical, some technical, some more artistic. His career has grown organically over time from web to motion graphics, from user interface to user experience. RST recently returned to Silicon Valley after leading Nike+ experience and innovation teams at R/GA New York as well as former key positions at Apple and Adobe.

He graduated from San Francisco State University with a BA in Graphic Communication and a minor in Computer Science. Ryan Scott currently resides in San Francisco with his wife and son, and when not thinking about design and technology he is an avid cyclist, marathoner, and doughnut connoisseur.

Sam Stringer-Hye

Senior Designer
Publicis Sapient
Brooklyn, New York
samstringerhye.com
linkedin.com/in/samstringerhye
instagram.com/samstringerhye
dribbble.com/samstringerhye

Originally from Nashville, Tennessee, I moved to New York City 6 years ago to pursue a career as a film editor. Since then my career has taken me down many diverse paths. I have created work for social media channels, online publishing, design agencies, and many more. Whether it's making things move or designing beautiful and practical digital products I am always thinking about core principles of design. You can find me glued to the latest Apple Keynote event.

Sarah Gray

Senior Creative Recruiter
Squarespace
Brooklyn, New York
squarespace.com

Sarah began her career in Recruiting as a Coordinator at an advertising agency in Boston, Massachusetts, shortly after graduating from college. As she started to take on a few open creative roles, she gravitated towards reviewing portfolios over resumes, and quickly learned that the subjectivity of each book was the best part. She currently works as a Senior Creative Recruiter at Squarespace in New York, focusing on hiring for roles within the Product Design and Brand Creative teams.

Sean King

Senior Web Designer
PVH Corporation
New York, New York
pvh.com
seankingdesign.com

Sean King started his design career in 1994 as a graphic designer at a screen printing shop. His experiences there fueled a hands-on approach to design that has informed his entire career. He has since designed for ad agencies and branding firms, has taught college design and typography classes, and currently works in the apparel industry. He served on the board of the Type Directors Club, and has presented at TypeCon.

Over the course of his career, he has designed items as varied as print ads, direct mail, point-of-sale displays, trade show displays, stage backdrops, multimedia presentations, logos, brand guidelines, newsletters, information graphics, books, typefaces, mobile apps, messaging animations, web ads, and websites.

Sean is based in New York City, where he has lived since 1995. He draws inspiration from the city's energy and multicultural atmosphere, as well as its rich design history.

Tadeu Magalhães

Senior Art Director
Huge
Brooklyn, New York
hugeinc.com
tadeumagalhaes.com

For 12 years, Tadeu has developed renowned brand identity projects, editorial pieces, and digital experiences for clients in various fields, ranging from tech, fashion, beauty, and real estate, to culture and the arts. Prior to joining Huge, Tadeu worked as the Design Director and Head of Print Production at RoAndCo for 7 years and produced work for brands such as Google, Estée Lauder, Shiseido, Refinery29, Honor, Creative Space, Monique Péan, Timo Weiland,

Svbscription, Rachael Ray, Bobbi Brown, and W Hotels. His branding and print projects have been awarded by Under Consideration's FPO Awards and Brand New Awards on multiple occasions and in 2014 he presented the talk "Fashion Branding: From Inspiration to Logo and Packaging" at The Dieline Conference.

Talia Brigneti
Interaction Designer
Google
San Francisco, California
google.com
talia.design

While my formal training in college (SCAD) was for Industrial Design, I organically transitioned into digital once I noticed the endless possibilities for innovation and impact in this space. At my current role, I am responsible for the UI and UX of products and systems within the Ads umbrella at Google. On my free time, I like to explore my artistic and active side by working on a new painting, exploring galleries or getting my heart rate up playing tennis!

Tim Sullivan
Designer at AREA 17
New York, New York
area17.com
timsullivan.work

Tim is a New York-based graphic designer who specializes in digital product design. His work is typographically driven and is characterized by clarity, directness, and a passionate attention to detail. He is a graduate of Bowdoin College and Massachusetts College of Art and Design. When not working in a grid, he can be found playing in one—a tennis court.

Tyler Wergin
Freelance Designer and Animator
New York, New York
tylerwergin.com
linkedin.com/in/tylerwergin
dribbble.com/tylerwergin

New York City-based freelance animator and designer. Graduated Full Sail University in 2014. A lover of all things design, with a passion for illustrative story-driven animation.

Wenkang Kan (Kevin Kan)
Visual Designer
Google
New York, New York
google.com
www.callmekevin.com

I'm Wenkang Kan, a New York City-based multidisciplinary designer and collaborator. An awards winner, a ramen enthusiast, and an illustrator. Working closely with teams, I tell stories, solve business problems, and connect people through digital products, branding, and interactive experiences. My proudest work includes Hawaiian Airline rebranding, Taco Bell logo, *New York Magazine* cover design, Google cloud media product, and more. My work is published in graphic design magazines including *Graphic*, *GDUSA*, and so on.

Yejee Pae
Junior Designer, Communal Creative, New York, New York
Class of 2018, BFA Design, School of Visual Arts, New York, New York
yejeepae.com
instagram.com/yejetables
linkedin.com/in/yejeepae

Yejee Pae (rhymes with veggie, edgy, or wedgie) is a Junior Designer at Communal Creative in New York. She was born and raised in Vancouver, Canada, and she currently lives in New York City. She graduated from the School of Visual Arts with a BFA in Design in 2018.

As a graphic designer, her strengths lie in activation designs that range from physical printed materials (which she loves most), packaging, web design, and animations. Away from the studio, she is a cat aunt (it's a thing), *Bon Appétit* wannabe chef, and will wiggle to funky music to relieve herself from a hard day's work of visual problem-solving.

About the author

Irina Lee is a Creative Director at Huge, a global digital agency in Brooklyn, New York. Irina leads a global team of user experience, visual designers, copywriters and developers across various portfolios of clients. Prior to Huge, she led product, service, retail, and experience design innovation for Nike, at R/GA in New York City. She worked with clients in technology, non-profits, education, culture, luxury, and retail, including Google, Nike, JP Morgan Chase, Verizon, United Technologies, Anheuser-Busch Inbev, Tiffany & Co., CHANEL, Jordan, Intuit, NYU, The City of New York, Brooklyn Public Library, Cities of Service, Bloomberg Philanthropies, and several others.

Outside of work, she teaches typography at the School of Visual Arts in New York City. She speaks 6 foreign languages and is a classically trained pianist. Irina founded First Person American, a story-telling initiative that uses film and multimedia to spark social change, which is a now a part of the Ellis Island Foundation. Her vision brought New York Welcoming Stories to life through filmmaking and storytelling workshops, public screenings and large scale events in partnership with major institutions such as the Welcoming America, New York City Immigrant Heritage Week, Ellis Island Foundation, Queens Museum of Art, The New York Public Library, Immigrant Movement, Facing History and Ourselves, Tenement Museum, and many others. She has won the Sappi Ideas that Matter grant, Adobe Foundation Design Ignites Change grant, Citizens Committee of New York grant, and the Facing History and Ourselves grant.

She received a Masters of Fine Art from the School of Visual Arts, a post-graduate certificate in Typeface Design from the Cooper Union, and a Bachelors of Art in Studio Art from the University of Maryland. Irina's typeface is part of the permanent collection at the Herb Lubalin Study Center of Design and Typography at Cooper Union in New York City.

Acknowledgments

I am forever grateful to my teachers and colleagues at the University of Maryland College Park, School of Visual Arts MFA Design, and Type@Cooper. You helped me become a better designer, writer, and educator.

Thank you to everyone at Bloomsbury. Lesley Ripley, who presented me with this incredible opportunity. Louise Baird-Smith, for helping shape this book. My heartfelt gratitude to the editor of this book, Felicity Cummins. The completion of this book would have been impossible without her support and guidance. Thank you to the entire team at Bloomsbury involved in the design and production of the book.

Thank you to all my students at the School of Visual Arts, and the State University of New York at Farmingdale. You are the reason this book exists, and I am proud to include your work in this publication.

A huge thanks goes out to all the contributors, for sharing your expertise and encouragement! To the colleagues at Huge and R/GA, you have built a digital design culture, and I am forever grateful to be a part of the ride.

Numerous designers and educators helped me along the way, including Sean King, Rietje Becker, Ashley Stevens, Lisa Maione.

Thank you to my friends who helped in guiding this book—Lara McCormick, Anna Nath, Nicole Kuang, and Danielle Filsinger—I'm grateful to have these inspiring women in my life.

I am grateful to my mom for her support, love, and wisdom.

My children, Avery and Everett, for inspiring me every day—keep learning, growing, and exploring the boundless possibilities around you.

Lastly, my best friend, and my loving husband, Adrian. Thank you for your endless inspiration.

Index